TEACHER'S PET PUBLICATIONS

LITPLAN TEACHER PACK
for
Mythology
based on the book by
Edith Hamilton

Written by
Barbara M. Linde, MA Ed.

© 2005 Teacher's Pet Publications
All Rights Reserved

Copyright Teacher's Pet Publications 2005

Only the student materials in this unit plan (such as worksheets, study questions, and tests) may be reproduced multiple times for use in the purchaser's classroom.

For any additional copyright questions, contact Teacher's Pet Publications.

www.tpet.com

TABLE OF CONTENTS - *Mythology*

Introduction	5
Unit Objectives	7
Unit Outline	8
Reading Assignment Sheet	9
Study Questions	13
Quiz/Study Questions (Multiple Choice)	35
Pre-Reading Vocabulary Worksheets	71
Lesson One (Introductory Lesson)	93
Nonfiction Assignment Sheet	105
Oral Reading Evaluation Form	102
Writing Assignment 1	97
Writing Evaluation Form	111
Writing Assignment 2	110
Writing Assignment 3	115
Extra Writing Assignments/Discussion ?s	98
Vocabulary Review Activities	119
Unit Review Activities	120
Unit Tests	127
Unit Resource Materials	161
Vocabulary Resource Materials	179

A FEW NOTES ABOUT THE AUTHOR
EDITH HAMILTON

HAMILTON, Edith 1867-1963 An American, Edith Hamilton was born in Dresden, Germany, on August 12, 1867. She grew up in Fort Wayne, Indiana. She was an avid reader from an early age, reading the works of Keats, Byron, and Shelley while still a child. She had an excellent memory, and often recited passages and entire poems to her family. Her father began teaching her Latin when she was seven years old.

While in college, Hamilton majored in classical studies. She earned a B.A. and an M.A. from Bryn Mawr College, completing her studies in 1895. She received a fellowship to study at the Universities of Leipzig and Munich, in Germany. Hamilton was the first woman to ever enroll at the University of Munich.

When she returned to the United States in 1896, she became the first headmistress of Bryn Mawr School in Baltimore. She based her theory of education on the Greek idea of emphasizing differences, and allowing each learner to develop his or her own talents. Hamilton kept the position as headmistress until she retired in 1922, at age 63. Upon her retirement, she purchased a house at Sea Wall, Mt. Desert Island, Maine.

Hamilton's career as a writer began in 1924, when she moved to New York City. In 1929 she took her first trip to Greece and Egypt. Her first book, *The Greek Way*, was published in 1930. In *The Greek Way*, she applied the Greek ideals of mind and spirit to modern civilization. This book established her reputation as a scholar. Following her first book, everything that she wrote for publication was accepted. In 1932 Hamilton published *The Roman Way*, which applied the works of the ancient poets to contemporary life.

Mythology was published in 1942, after three years of hard work. This retelling of Greek, Roman, and Norse mythology was well-received, and sold more than one and a half million copies. Hamilton subsequently published *Witness to the Truth: Christ and His Interpreters* in 1948, and *The Echo of Greece* in 1957. In addition, she wrote several magazine articles and reviews, and translated classics from the original Greek.

Athens, Greece, awarded her honorary citizenship in 1957. By this time she was also recognized as the greatest woman classicist. Hamilton continued writing, traveling, and lecturing until 1962, when she was in her mid-nineties. She died on May 31, 1963.

INTRODUCTION - *Mythology*

This unit has been designed to develop students' reading, writing, thinking, listening and speaking skills through exercises and activities related to *Mythology* by Edith Hamilton. It includes twenty-one lessons, supported by extra resource materials.

The **introductory lesson** introduces students to the concept that mythology shows us the way the human race thought and felt ages ago. Students will be encouraged to relate the knowledge they already have about mythology to the stories in the book.

The **reading assignments** are approximately thirty pages each; some are a little shorter while others are a little longer. Students have approximately 15 minutes of pre-reading work to do prior to each reading assignment. This pre-reading work involves reviewing the study questions for the assignment and doing some vocabulary work for 8 to 10 vocabulary words they will encounter in their reading.

The **study guide questions** are fact-based questions; students can find the answers to these questions right in the text. These questions come in two formats: short answer or multiple choice. The best use of these materials is probably to use the short answer version of the questions as study guides for students (since answers will be more complete), and to use the multiple choice version for occasional quizzes. It might be a good idea to make transparencies of your answer keys for the overhead projector.

The **vocabulary work** is intended to enrich students' vocabularies as well as to aid in the students' understanding of the book. Prior to each reading assignment, students will complete a two-part worksheet for approximately 8 to 10 vocabulary words in the upcoming reading assignment. Part I focuses on students' use of general knowledge and contextual clues by giving the sentence in which the word appears in the text. Students are then to write down what they think the words mean based on the words' usage. Part II gives students dictionary definitions of the words and has them match the words to the correct definitions based on the words' contextual usage. Students should then have an understanding of the words when they meet them in the text.

After each reading assignment, students will go back and formulate answers for the study guide questions. Discussion of these questions serves as a **review** of the most important events and ideas presented in the reading assignments.

After students complete extra discussion questions, there is a **vocabulary review** lesson which pulls together all the separate vocabulary lists for the reading assignments and gives students a review of all of the words they have studied.

Following the reading of the book, two lessons are devoted to the **extra discussion questions/writing assignments.** These questions focus on interpretation, critical analysis and personal response, employing a variety of thinking skills and adding to the students' understanding of the novel. These questions are done as a **group activity**. Using the information they have acquired so far through individual work and class discussions, students get together to further examine the text and to brainstorm ideas relating to the themes of the book.

The group activity is followed by a **reports and discussion** session in which the groups share their ideas about the book with the entire class; thus, the entire class gets exposed to many different ideas regarding the themes and events of the book.

There are three **writing assignments** in this unit, each with the purpose of informing, persuading, or having students express personal opinions. The first assignment is to express a **personal opinion** about some aspect of the book. Students will be assigned a question from the Extra Writing Assignments and/or Discussion Questions pages to answer. The second assignment is to give **information**. Students will create travelogues that describe journeys they have taken. The third writing assignment is writing to **persuade**. Students will adopt the role of defense or prosecuting attorney and deliver a final argument pertaining to the punishment Prometheus received from Zeus.

In addition, there is a **nonfiction reading assignment**. Students are required to read a piece of nonfiction related in some way to *Mythology*. After reading their nonfiction pieces, students will fill out a worksheet on which they answer questions regarding facts, interpretation, criticism, and personal opinions. During one class period, students make **oral presentations** about the nonfiction pieces they have read. This not only exposes all students to a wealth of information, it also gives students the opportunity to practice **public speaking.**

The **review lesson** pulls together all of the aspects of the unit. The teacher is given four or five choices of activities or games to use which all serve the same basic function of reviewing all of the information presented in the unit.

The **unit test** comes in two formats: all multiple choice-matching-true/false or a mixture of matching, short answer, and composition. As a convenience, two different tests for each format have been included.

There are additional **support materials** included with this unit. The **Unit Resource Section** includes suggestions for an in-class library, crossword and word search puzzles related to the novel, and extra vocabulary worksheets. There is a list of **bulletin board ideas** which gives the teacher suggestions for bulletin boards to go along with this unit. In addition, there is a list of **extra class activities** the teacher could choose from to enhance the unit or as a substitution for an exercise the teacher might feel is inappropriate for his/her class. **Answer keys** are located directly after the **reproducible student materials** throughout the unit. The student materials may be reproduced for use in the teacher's classroom without infringement of copyrights. No other portion of this unit may be reproduced without the written consent of Teacher's Pet Publications, Inc.

UNIT OBJECTIVES *Mythology*

1. Through reading *Mythology* students will study Hamilton's interpretation of Greek, Roman, and Norse mythology.

2. Students will gain an understanding of the ancient Greek, Roman, and Norse concepts of creation and the early development of mankind.

3. Students will study the techniques of summarizing and retelling stories.

4. Students will practice reading aloud and silently to improve their skills in each area.

5. Students will answer questions to demonstrate their knowledge and understanding of the main events and characters in *Mythology*.

6. Students will demonstrate their understanding of the text on four levels: factual, interpretive, critical, and personal.

7. Students will define their own viewpoints based on their understanding.

8. Students will enrich their vocabularies and improve their understanding of the text through the vocabulary lessons prepared for use in conjunction with text.

9. The writing assignments in this unit are geared to several purposes:
    a. To have students demonstrate their abilities to inform, to persuade, or to express their own personal ideal
        Note: Students will demonstrate ability to write effectively by developing and organizing facts to convey information. Students will demonstrate the ability to write effectively to persuade by selecting and organizing relevant information, establishing an argumentative purpose, and by designing an appropriate strategy for an identified audience. Students will demonstrate the ability to write effectively to express personal ideas by selecting a form and its appropriate elements.
    b. To check the students' reading comprehension
    c. To make students think about the ideas presented in the text
    d. To encourage critical and logical thinking
    e. To provide the opportunity to practice good grammar and improve students' use of the English language

10. Students will read aloud, report, and participate in large and small group discussions to improve their public speaking and personal interaction skills.

READING ASSIGNMENT SHEET *Mythology*

DATE ASSIGNED	CHAPTERS	COMPLETION DATE
	Introduction, Part One: Chapters 1-2	
	Part One: Chapters 3-4	
	Part Two: Chapters 5-6	
	Part Two: Chapters 7-8	
	Part Three: Chapters 9-12	
	Part Four: Chapters 13-14	
	Part Four: Chapters 15-16	
	Part Five: Chapters 17-19	
	Part Six: Chapters 20-21	
	Part Seven: Introduction & 22-23	

UNIT OUTLINE *Mythology*

1 Unit Intro Writing Assignment 1	2 PVR Intro & Chapters 1-2	3 Study ??s PVR Chapters 3-4	4 Nonfiction Assignment Library Work	5 Study ?s PVR 5-6 Assign 7-12
6 PVR 7-8	7 Study ??s 9-12	8 Quiz 1-12 PVR 13-14	9 Study ??s 13-14 PVR 15-16	10 Study ??s 15-16 Discussion
11 Writing Assignment 2	12 PVR 17-19	13 Writing Conferences	14 PVR 20-21	15 Writing Assignment 3
16 PVR Part Seven	17 Group Work	18 Extra Discussion ??s	19 Non-Fiction Discussion	20 Vocabulary Review
21 Review	22 Test			

Key: P = Preview Study Questions   V = Vocabulary Work   R = Read

STUDY GUIDE QUESTIONS

SHORT ANSWER STUDY GUIDE QUESTIONS *Mythology*

<u>Introduction</u>
1. What is the purpose of Greek and Roman mythology?
2. What is the first written record of Greece called, and who was the author?
3. What do the myths show us about the early Greeks?
4. Why did the portrayal of Zeus change over the years?
5. What is the *Theogony*, and why is it important?

Part One *The Gods, The Creation, and The Earliest Heroes*

<u>Chapter 1 *The Gods*</u>   <u>Chapter 2 *The Two Great Gods of Earth*</u>
1. What did the Greeks believe about the origins of the gods and the universe?
2. Who were the first parents, and who were their children and grandchildren?
3. How did Homer describe Olympus?
4. Give the Roman names for the following gods and goddesses: Zeus, Hades, Artemis, Hermes, Hestia.
5. Give the Greek names for these gods and goddesses: Juno, Neptune, Minerva, Venus, Mars, Vulcan.
6. How was the will of Zeus revealed at the oracle at Dodona?
7. Describe the breastplate, bird, and tree that symbolize Zeus.
8. What was the dual relationship between Zeus and Hera?
9. Describe Hera's personality.
10. Who were Zeus' two brothers, and where did they rule?
11. Briefly describe the characteristics and functions of any two of the following gods and goddesses: Athena, Phoebus Apollo, Artemis, or Aphrodite.
12. Briefly describe the characteristics and functions of any two of the following gods and goddesses: Hermes, Hephaestus, Hestia, Cupid, Ares, or the Muses and Graces.
13. What did Hermes have on his feet, hat, and wand, and why?
14. Name the Gods of the Waters.
15. Who are the main gods of the Underworld?
16. What are the Elysian Fields?
17. Briefly retell the story of Demeter (Ceres).
18. What were the two central ideas in the worship of Dionysus?
19. Why did Dionysus become the center of the belief in immortality?
20. How were Demeter and Dionysus different from the other gods and goddesses?

Short Answer Study Guide Questions-*Mythology*
Part One *The Gods, The Creation, and The Earliest Heroes* continued

Chapter 3 *How the World and Mankind Were Created*   Chapter 4 *The Earliest Heroes*
1. What did the Greeks think was at the very beginning of things?
2. What were the next six creations, in order?
3. Who was Cronus, and why was he significant?
4. How did Zeus become the ruler of heaven and earth?
5. Describe the Greek concept of the geography of the Earth.
6. Briefly retell the story of Prometheus's creation of mankind.
7. Who was Pandora, and why was she created?
8. Briefly retell the story of Pandora's box.
9. Why did Zeus punish Prometheus, and how did he do this?
10. Who was Io?
11. Briefly retell the story of Europa.
12. Briefly retell te story of Polyphemus.
13. What is the story of Narcissus?
14. Who was Echo?
15. What is the story of Adonis?

Part Two *Stories of Love and Adventure*

Chapter 5 *Cupid and Psyche*   Chapter 6 *Eight Brief Tales of Lovers*
1. Why was Venus angry at Psyche?
2. Was Venus's plan for revenge successful?
3. What did Psyche discover about her mysterious husband, and what happened when she discovered it?
4. What finally happened to Cupid and Psyche?
5. Which lovers arranged a tryst, mistakenly thought the other had been killed, and killed themselves?
6. Identify the lovers in the following summary. He was the son of one of the Muses, and a gifted musician. She died on their wedding day. He went to the underworld and tried, unsuccessfully, to bring her back.
7. This man was killed at sea. Morpheus appeared to his wife and told her that her husband was dead. Then she and her dead husband were turned into birds.
8. He fell in love with a statue that he had made. Venus brought the statue to life and they married. Who were they?
9. What did Baucis and Philemon do?
10. Apollo fell in love with this daughter of the river god Peneus. She did not love him. To protect her, her father turned her into a laurel tree. Who was this?

Short Answer Study Guide Questions - *Mythology*

Part Two *Stories of Love and Adventure* continued
Chapter 7 *The Quest of the Golden Fleece*   Chapter 8 *Four Great Adventures*

1. Why was Jason's journey significant?
2. What was the origin of the Golden Fleece?
3. Why did Jason undertake the search for the Golden Fleece?
4. What were the Harpies, and how were they destroyed?
5. Name Jason's ship and at least one of the heroes who traveled with him.
6. Who were the Amazons?
7. What task did Jason have to perform for King AEetes in order to get the Golden Fleece?
8. Who helped Jason, and why?
9. Who were Pegasus and Bellerophon?
10. Which father and son used wings made by the father to escape from the Labyrinth, and were they successful?

Part Three *The Great Heroes Before the Trojan War*
Chapter 9 *Perseus*   Chapter 10 *Theseus*   Chapter 11 *Hercules*   Chapter 12 *Atalanta*

1. What was the Medusa, and how did Perseus kill it?
2. How did Perseus use Medusa's head to help his mother?
3. Theseus was raised in a city away from his father, King Aegeus of Athens. How did the King know that Theseus was his son when they finally met?
4. What was the Minotaur, and how did Theseus kill it?
5. How did Theseus change the government when he became King of Athens?
6. Who was the strongest man on earth, and the great hero of Greece except for Athens?
7. Why did Hercules perform his twelve labors?
8. Briefly describe one of the twelve labors of Hercules.
9. Whom did Atalanta tell her father she would marry?
10. Whom did Atalanta marry, and how did he win her?

Part Four *The Heroes of the Trojan War*
Chapter 13 *The Trojan War*   Chapter 14 *The Fall of Troy*

1. From which source did Hamilton take most of the story of the Trojan War?
2. What was the Judgment of Paris?
3. What was the cause of the Trojan War?
4. Who were the main combatants and gods on the Greek side?
5. Who were the main combatants on the Trojan side?
6. Who was killed during the battle between Achilles and Hector?
7. How was Achilles killed?
8. What did Diomedes steal from the city of Troy, and why?
9. How did the Greeks finally get into Troy?
10. Which of the Trojans escaped, and who helped them?

Short Answer Study Guide Questions-*Mythology*

Part Four *The Heroes of the Trojan War* continued
Chapter 15 *The Adventures of Odysseus*   Chapter 16 *The Adventures of Aeneas*

1. From which mythology source did Edith Hamilton take the adventures of Odysseus?
2. What caused Athena to become angry at the Greeks?
3. How did Poseidon avenge Athena?
4. What was happening with Penelope, wife of Odysseus, while he was trying to get home?
5. Who was Telemachus, and what did he do?
6. How did the Phaeacians help Odysseus?
7. What happened to Odysseus and his men when they reached Circe's island?
8. Where did Odysseus have to go to find out how to get home?
9. How did Odysseus get rid of the suitors when he arrived home?
10. What is the source for the adventures of Aeneas?
11. Why did Aeneas go on a journey?
12. Who was Dido, and why was she important?
13. What role did Juno and Venus have in the story of Aeneas?
14. Where did Aeneas go when he left Carthage?
15. Briefly describe the war in Italy.

Part Five *The Great Families of Mythology*
Chapter 17 *The House of Atreus*   Chapter 18 *The House of Thebes*
Chapter 19 *The Royal House of Athens*

1. Name two of the members of the house of Atreus.
2. Who brought all of the misfortunes on the house of Atreus?
3. What was the evil deed Tantalus committed?
4. What punishment did Tantalus receive for this deed?
5. What did Tantalus's daughter, Niobe, do, and how was she punished?
6. Why had Agamemnon killed his daughter Iphigenia?
7. How did Agamemnon die?
8. What happened to Clytemnestra and her lover, Aegisthus?
9. What one good thing resulted from Orestes's repentance?
10. What did Cadmus do?
11. What happened to Cadmus and Harmonia, and what did this show?
12. What wrongs did Oedipus commit?
13. Did he commit this crime knowingly?
14. What punishment did Oedipus inflict upon himself?
15. Why was Antigone killed?
16. How did Theseus, King of Athens, help Adrastus and the relatives of the chieftains who fought against Thebes?
17. For what was Cecrops noted?
18. How did Philomela let Procne know of Tereus's evil deeds?
19. What happened to Procne and Philomela?
20. How did Cephalus test Procris's devotion to him?
21. How were Creusa and Ion reunited?

Short Answer Study Guide Questions-*Mythology*

Part Six *The Less Important Myths*
Chapter 20 *Midas and Others*   Chapter 21 *Brief Myths*

1. What wish did Bacchus grant to Midas, and what was the result?
2. For what was Aesculapius honored?
3. What wrong did the Danaids do, and what was their punishment?
4. What was Arachne's misdeed, and what was her punishment?
5. Which human lover of Zeus' was changed into the Great Bear and placed in the sky?
6. For what was the centaur Chiron known?
7. Why were the Myrmidons created?
8. Which great hunter was placed in the sky as a constellation?
9. Who were the Pleiades?
10. What did Sisyphus do, and how was he punished?

Part Seven *The Mythology of the Norsemen*
Introduction Chapter 22 *The Stories of Signy and Sigurd* Chapter 23 *The Norse Gods*

1. What was Asgard like?
2. What was the Norse outlook on good and evil?
3. What was the choice the Norse hero made?
4. What was the central theme of the Norse mythology?
5. Briefly retell the story of Signy and Sigmund.
6. Whom did Sigurd rescue?
7. How does Sigurd die?
8. How did Balder die?
9. Describe Odin and his duties.
10. Who were the Valkyries?
11. Which days of the week were named after Norse gods?
12. Who ruled the Kingdom of Death?
13. How did Odin and his brothers make the world?
14. Who was the Thunder-god?
15. Who was Odin's wife?
16. Who was Tyr?
17. Who was the Goddess of Love and Beauty?
18. What was Midgard?
19. What did the Norsemen believe would happen after Odin and the other gods were defeated by evil?
20. What, according to Hamilton, were the Norsemen's two characteristics?

SHORT ANSWER STUDY GUIDE QUESTIONS ANSWER KEY *Mythology*

<u>Introduction</u>
1. What is the purpose of Greek and Roman mythology?
    The myths tell us the way the human race thought and felt ages ago.

2. What is the first written record of Greece called, and who was the author?
    It is the *Iliad*, written by Homer.

3. What do the myths show us about the early Greeks?
    The myths show us how much the early Greeks had progressed from primitive man.

4. Why did the portrayal of Zeus change over the years?
    As man matured, he became more conscious of the demands of life, and of what humans needed in their gods.

5. What is the *Theogony*, and why is it important?
    It is an account of the creation of the universe and the gods, and is important to mythology.

Part One The Gods, the Creation, and the Earliest Heroes
<u>Chapter 1 The Gods Chapter 2 The Two Great Gods of Earth</u>

1. What did the Greeks believe about the origins of the gods and the universe?
    The Greeks believed that the universe created the gods.

2. Who were the first parents, and who were their children and grandchildren?
    Heaven and Earth were the first parents. The Titans (Cronus-Saturn, Ocean, Tethys, Hyperion, Mnemosyne, Themis, and Iapetus) were their children, the gods were their grandchildren.

3. How did Homer describe Olympus?
    Homer described Olympus as a mysterious region far above the mountains, but it was not heaven.

4. Give the Roman names for the following gods and goddesses: Zeus, Hades, Artemis, Hermes, Hestia.
    Zeus = Jupiter; Hades = Pluto; Artemis = Diana; Hermes = Mercury; Hestia = Vesta

5. Give the Greek names for these gods and goddesses: Juno, Neptune, Minerva, Venus, Mars, Vulcan.
    Juno = Hera; Neptune = Poseidon; Minerva = Pallas Athena; Venus = Aphrodite; Mars = Ares; Vulcan = Hephaestus.

6. How was the will of Zeus revealed at the oracle at Dodona?
    The priests at the oracle interpreted the rustling of the oak leaves.

Part One Chapters 1 & 2 continued
7. Describe the breastplate, bird, and tree that symbolized Zeus.
    The breastplate was the aegis, his bird was the eagle, and the oak was his tree.

8. What was the dual relationship between Zeus and Hera?
    Hera was both the wife and sister of Zeus.

9. Describe Hera's personality.
    She was the protector of marriage. She was usually portrayed as angry and vindictive,
     mostly toward the many human females with whom Zeus fell in love.

10. Who were Zeus' two brothers and where did they rule?
    Poseidon (Neptune) ruled the sea, and Hades (Pluto) ruled the underworld and the dead.

11. Briefly describe the characteristics and functions of any two of the following gods and goddesses:
    Athena, Phoebus Apollo, Artemis, or Aphrodite.
    Athena sprang full grown from the head of Zeus. She was the protector of civilized life.
    She invented the bridle, and was the first to tame horses for men's use. She was known as
    the Maiden, or Parthenos, and her temple was the Parthenon. Athena symbolized
    wisdom, reason, and purity.

    Phoebus Apollo played the golden lyre, and was also the Archer and Healer. His oracle at
    Delphi was a direct link between gods and men.

    Artemis (Diana) was the Huntsman.

    Aphrodite (Venus) was the Goddess of Love and Beauty.

12. Briefly describe the characteristics and functions of any two of the following gods and
    goddesses: Hephaestus, Hestia, Cupid, Ares, or The Muses and Graces.
    Hephaestus (Vulcan) was the God of Fire. He made the armor and furniture for the gods.
    He was also the patron of handicrafts and the protector of smiths.

    Hestia (Vesta) was Zeus' sister and the Goddess of the Hearth. She does not play an
    important part in the myths, although offerings were made to her in all homes.

    Cupid (Eros) was the God of Love. The later poets said he was Aphrodite's son.

      Ares (Mars) was the God of War.

      There were nine Muses, the daughters of Zeus and Memory. They were known for their singing, and each also had a special field. There were three Graces: Splendor, Mirth, and Good Cheer. They were always together.

13. What did Hermes have on his feet, hat, and wand, and why?
    Hermes (Mercury) was the messenger of the gods. He had winged sandals on his feet, wings on his hat and magic wand.

14. Name the Gods of the Waters.
    Poseidon (Neptune) was the ruler of the waters. Ocean, a Titan, was Lord of the River Ocean. Nereus was the Old Man of the Sea. Triton used a shell as a trumpet. Proteus could change his shape at will. The Naiads were water nymphs.

15. Who were the main gods of the Underworld?
    Hades (Pluto) ruled the Underworld. His Queen was Persephone. Charon ferried the souls of the dead across the water, where the three-headed, dragon-tailed dog, Cerberus, guarded the gate. The Furies punished evildoers. Sleep, Death, and Dreams also lived in the underworld.

16. What were the Elysian Fields?
    They were a place of blessedness in the underworld where those who were good in life went.

17. Briefly retell the story of Demeter (Ceres).
    Demeter was the Goddess of the Corn. Her daughter, Persephone, was carried off to the underworld by Hades. Demeter was greatly upset, and no crops grew on the earth. Zeus then ruled that Persephone would spend four months of every year in the underworld, and the rest of the time on the earth with her mother. The crops grew and flowers bloomed while Persephone was on the earth, but all died when she went to the underworld.

18. What were the two central ideas in the worship of Dionysus?
    Dionysus was the God of the Vine. He could give either joy or savage brutality, because wine could be both bad and good.

19. Why did Dionysus become the center of the belief in immortality?
    He was the symbol of the vine, which is pruned every year, and then grows back in the spring. His followers believed that his death and resurrection indicate the eternal life of the soul.

20. How were Demeter and Dionysus different from the other gods and goddesses?
    They were the only ones who knew suffering, as the mortals did.

Part One *The Gods, the Creation, and the Earliest Heroes*
Chapter 3 <u>*How the World and Mankind Were Created*</u> Chapter 4 <u>*The Earliest Heroes*</u>

1. What did the Greeks think was at the very beginning of things?
   They thought Chaos, or formless confusion, was at the very beginning.

2. What were the next six creations, in order?
   Night and Erebus, the children of Chaos, were created next. They created Love, who created Light and Day. Then Earth was created, although the method was never explained.

3. Who was Cronus, and why was he significant?
   Cronus was a Titan. He wounded his father, Heaven, and became Lord of the Universe. Cronus ate five of his six children because he knew that one of them would one day dethrone him.

4. How did Zeus become the ruler of heaven and earth?
   His mother, Rhea, hid Zeus from Cronus when he was born. When Zeus was grown he forced Cronus to disgorge his five siblings. Zeus and his brothers warred against Cronus and the Titans. Zeus eventually mastered the use of thunder and lightning, his brother and sister gods became more powerful, and they defeated Cronus and the Titans.

5. Describe the Greek concept of the geography of the Earth.
   The Greeks thought the Earth was a round disk divided into two parts by the Sea. The great river, Ocean, flowed around the Earth. The land of the dead was on Ocean's bank.

6. Briefly retell the story of Prometheus's creation of mankind.
   Prometheus created mankind after his brother created the animals. He gave man an upright shape like the gods. To protect them, Prometheus gave men the gift of fire.

7. Who was Pandora, and why was she created?
   Pandora means "the gift of all." She was the first woman, and was lovely. Zeus created her to punish mankind for tricking him into accepting the fat and bones of any sacrificial animals. He intended Pandora, and all subsequent women, to be beautiful, but an evil to men.

8. Briefly retell the story of Pandora's box.
   The gods gave Pandora a box full of harmful things, and told her not to open it. She was curious and lifted the lid. All of the troubles of the world flew out. Hope also came out of the box.

9. Why did Zeus punish Prometheus, and how did he do this?
    Prometheus had stolen fire for mankind, and had also arranged for them to receive the best part of sacrificial animals. Prometheus was also the only one who knew who would be the mother of the son who would dethrone Zeus. Zeus had his servants, Force and Violence, bind Prometheus to a rock. Every day an eagle would come down and eat Prometheus's liver. Prometheus never gave in, but he was eventually released.

10. Who was Io?
    Io was a maiden with whom Zeus fell in love. He turned her into a calf to fool Hera, and was forced to leave her that way. Eventually she was returned to human form. Hercules was a direct descendent of Io.

11. Briefly retell the story of Europa.
    Europa was a beautiful maiden. Aphrodite and Cupid shot Zeus with an arrow and made him fall in love with Europa. He changed into a bull and carried her away from her home to the island of Crete. The sons of Europa and Zeus became famous.

12. Briefly retell the story of Polyphemus.
    Polyphemus was the Cyclops whom Odysseus encountered on his way home from the Trojan War. Polyphemus was fierce and ill-natured. He captured Odysseus and his men in his cave and ate several of them. Odysseus and his men got Polyphemus drunk and put out his one eye with a red-hot spike. They escaped from the cave by tying themselves to the undersides of Polyphemus' rams. Polyphemus could feel along the backs of the rams when they left his cave, but he could not tell that the men were holding on underneath.

13. What is the story of Narcissus?
    Narcissus was a beautiful lad who refused to fall in love with any maiden. The goddess Nemesis made him fall in love with his reflection in a pool. He would not look away from his reflection, and so he died. A lovely flower bloomed on the spot where he died, and it was named after him.

14. Who was Echo?
    Echo was a nymph. Hera punished her unjustly by condemning her to only be able to repeat what was said. Echo was in love with Narcissus, but was not able to tell him so. She wasted away, and only her voice was left.

15. What is the story of Adonis?
    Aphrodite and Persephone were both in love with Adonis. Zeus declared that he should spend half of the year with each of them. One day while he was hunting he was gored by a boar and died. The red flowers called anemones bloomed on his drops of blood.

Part Two *Stories of Love and Adventure*
Chapter 5 *Cupid and Psyche*   Chapter 6 *Eight Brief Tales of Lovers*

1. Why was Venus angry at Psyche?
    Psyche was the loveliest maiden alive. Many mortals began worshipping her and forgot Venus. This angered the goddess and she planned to punish Psyche.

2. Was Venus' plan for revenge successful?
    No, it wasn't. Cupid fell in love with her himself.

3. What did Psyche discover about her mysterious husband, and what happened when she discovered it?
    She discovered that Cupid was her husband. He fled from her when she saw him. She had betrayed his trust by looking at him after she had promised not to.

4. What finally happened to Cupid and Psyche?
    They were married in Olympus. Zeus made Psyche a goddess. Love and the Soul were together forever.

5. Which lovers arranged a tryst, mistakenly thought the other had been killed, and killed themselves?
    They were Pyramus and Thisbe.

6. Identify the lovers in the following summary. He was the son of one of the Muses, and a gifted musician. She died on their wedding day. He went to the underworld and tried unsuccessfully to bring her back.
    They were Orpheus and Eurydice.

7. This man was killed at sea. Morpheus appeared to his wife in the form of her dead husband and told her that her husband was dead. Then she and her dead husband were turned into birds.
    They were Ceyx and Alcyone.

8. He fell in love with a statue that he had made. Venus brought the statue to life and they married. Who were they?
    They were Pygmalion and Galatea.

9. What did Baucis and Philemon do?
    They gave hospitality to Jupiter and Mercury when they came to earth in disguise.

10. Apollo fell in love with this daughter of the river god, Peneus. She did not love him. To protect her, her father turned her into a laurel tree. Who was this?
    It was Daphne.

Part Two Stories of Love and Adventure
Chapter 7 <u>The Quest of the Golden Fleece</u>   Chapter 8 <u>Four Great Adventures</u>

1. Why was Jason's journey significant?
    Jason was the first hero in Europe who went on a great journey.

2. What was the origin of the Golden Fleece?
    Hermes had sent a golden ram to save a young prince, Phrixus, from being sacrificed at the altar. Later, Phrixus sacrificed the ram to Zeus and gave the Golden Fleece to King Aeetes.

3. Why did Jason undertake the search for the Golden Fleece?
    Jason was trying to regain the kingdom that had been taken from his father by a cousin. The cousin agreed to give it back if Jason could bring him the Golden Fleece. Jason loved adventure, and set off in his ship, the *Argo*, to find the Fleece.

4. What were the Harpies, and what happened to them?
    The Harpies were flying creatures who had a terrible smell. They were defiling the food of an old prophet. The sons of the North Wind, who were traveling with Jason, offered to kill them. Iris, the rainbow messenger of the gods, promised that they would do no more harm harm if they were allowed to live. The brothers agreed.

5. Name Jason's ship and at least one of the heroes who traveled with him.
    His ship was the *Argo*. Among the travelers were Hercules, twins Castor and Pollux, Orpheus, and Peleus, father of Achilles.

6. Who were the Amazons?
    They were the daughters of Harmony and Ares. They were fierce warriors.

7. What task did Jason have to perform for King Aetes in order to get the Golden Fleece?
    Jason yoked two fierce bulls together and used them to plow a field. Then he sowed dragon's teeth in the field. Next he killed the armed warriors who sprang up from the dragon's teeth.

8. Who helped Jason, and why?
    Medea, the daughter of King Aetes did. She was a powerful magician and gave him charms to use. She did this because Cupid had made her fall in love with Jason.

9. Who were Pegasus and Bellerophon?
   Bellerophon was a son of Poseidon and a mortal woman. He lived in Corinth. His only wish was to ride Pegasus, the winged horse. Athena helped him. When he tried to ride to Olympus, Pegasus threw him. After that he wandered the earth.

10. Which father and son used wings made by the father to escape from the Labyrinth, and were they successful?
    Daedalus was the father, and Icarus the son. They escaped, but then Icarus flew too close to the sun and the glue on the wings melted. He fell into the sea. Daedalus escaped to Sicily.

Part Three The Great Heroes Before the Trojan War
Chapter 9 *Perseus*   Chapter 10 *Theseus*   Chapter 11 *Hercules*   Chapter 12 *Atalanta*

1. What was the Medusa, and how did Perseus kill it?
   Medusa was a Gorgon, with hair made of snakes. Anyone who looked at her would turn to stone. Perseus was helped by Athena and Hermes. He used Hermes's sword and Athena's shield. He looked into the shield at Medusa's reflection and cut off her head.

2. How did Perseus kill his grandfather?
   He threw a discus that accidentally swerved and killed his grandfather.

3. Theseus was raised in a city away from his father, King Aegeus of Athens. How did the King know that Theseus was his son when they finally met?
   Aegeus had placed a sword and a pair of shoes in a hollow below a great stone. He told his wife that when the boy was strong enough to get the items, he should come with them to Athens. Theseus did this, and Aegeus recognized Theseus as his son.

4. What was the Minotaur, and how did Theseus kill it?
   The Minotaur was half bull, half human, the son of King Minos of Crete. It lived in the Labyrinth made by Daedalus. Every nine years fourteen young Athenians were sacrificed to it. Theseus volunteered to be sacrificed. The King's daughter, Ariadne, gave him a ball of thread which he unwound as he went through the Labyrinth. He killed the Minotaur with his bare hands and followed the string out of the Labyrinth.

5. How did Theseus change the government when he became King of Athens?
   He established a government by the people, where all were equal. He organized a commonwealth, resigned the throne, and became the Commander in Chief. Athens became the only really free state in the world at that time.

6. Who was the strongest man on earth, and the great hero of the rest of Greece (except Athens?)
    This was Hercules. He was the son of Zeus and Alcmena, a mortal.

7. Why did Hercules perform his twelve labors?
    Hera had made him mad. He killed his wife and children. When he came out of his madness he wanted to do penance for his deeds. His cousin, King Eurystheus, gave him the twelve labors.

8. Briefly describe one of the twelve labors of Hercules.
    (TEACHERS, ALL LABORS ARE SUMMARIZED HERE FOR YOU.)
    1) He killed the lion of Nemea by choking it.
    2) He killed the nine-headed Hydra.
    3) He brought back alive a stag with golden horns.
    4) He captured a great boar.
    5) He cleaned the very dirty Augean stables by diverting two rivers and making them flood the stables.
    6) He shot the birds that plagued the people of Stymphalus.
    7) He took a bull that belonged to Minos of Crete.
    8) He killed King Diomedes, and took his man-eating mare.
    9) He stole the girdle of Hippolyta, Queen of the Amazons. He killed her in the process.
    10) He brought back the cattle of Geryon.
    11) He brought back the Golden Apples of the Hesperides. He held the vault of heaven for Atlas so that Atlas could find the apples for him. Then he tricked Atlas into taking the heavens back onto his own shoulders.
    12) He went to the underworld and freed Theseus from the Chair of Forgetfulness.

9. Whom did Atalanta tell her father she would marry?
    She said she would marry the man who could beat her in a foot race.

10. Whom did Atalanta marry, and how did he win her?
    His name was either Melanion or Hippomenes. Aphrodite gave him three irresistible golden apples. During the race, he threw them, one at a time, near Atalanta. She stopped to get each of them and he beat her to the finish line.

Part Four *The Heroes of the Trojan War*
Chapter 13 *The Trojan War*   Chapter 14 *The Fall of Troy*

1. From which source did Hamilton take most of the story of the Trojan War?
    She took it from the *Iliad* by Homer.

2. What was the Judgment of Paris?
    Paris was the son of King Priam of Troy. The goddesses Hera, Aphrodite, and Pallas Athena were feuding over who was the fairest, and would become the owner of the golden apple. They asked Paris to listen to each of their bribes and choose who would get the apple. He liked Aphrodite's bribe, that the fairest woman in the world would be his. He awarded her the Golden Apple.

3. What was the cause of the Trojan War?
    Aphrodite took Paris to the most beautiful woman in the world. She was Helen, who lived in Greece and was married to King Menelaus of Sparta. Paris took her back to Troy with him. All of Helen's former suitors allied with Menelaus to get her back. This was the start of the Trojan War.

4. Who were the main combatants and gods on the Greek side?
    They were Menelaus, Odysseus, Achilles, and Agamemnon. Hera, Athena, and Poseidon favored the Greeks.

5. Who were the main combatants on the Trojan side?
    They were Paris and Hector. Aphrodite, Ares, Apollo, and Artemis were on the Trojans' side. Zeus favored them but tried to remain neutral.

6. Who was killed during the battle between Achilles and Hector?
    Hector was killed.

7. How was Achilles killed?
    Paris shot an arrow at him. Apollo guided the arrow to Achilles' heel, which was his only vulnerable spot.

8. What did Diomedes steal from the city of Troy, and why?
    He stole the sacred image of Pallas Athena. Supposedly Troy could not be conquered as long as it was in the city.

9. How did the Greeks finally get into Troy?
    Odysseus had a huge wooden horse built. He and several of the chieftains hid inside it. The Trojans took the horse into the city. That night the Greeks snuck out of the horse and massacred the Trojans.

10. Which of the Trojans escaped, and who helped them?
    Aphrodite helped Aeneas, his father, and his son to escape. She also took Helen to Menelaus.

Part Four *The Heroes of the Trojan War*
Chapter 15 *The Adventures of Odysseus*   Chapter 16 *The Adventures of Aeneas*

1. From which mythology source did Edith Hamilton take the adventures of Odysseus?
    The source is *The Odyssey*, by Homer. It is the companion book to *The Iliad*.

2. What caused Athena to become angry at the Greeks?
    The Greeks found a prophetess, Cassandra, in Athena's temple in Troy. They dragged her out. Athena was furious at this sacrilege. She asked Poseidon to help her take revenge on the Greeks.

3. How did Poseidon avenge Athena?
    He caused a great tempest in the sea. The Greek fleet was scattered, and many men drowned. Odysseus remained alive, but was shipwrecked.

4. What was happening with Penelope, wife of Odysseus, while he was trying to get home?
    Many men were courting her. She was doing her best to avoid marrying any of them. The suitors were rude, and were eating all of her food, but she still held out hope that her husband would return.

5. Who was Telemachus, and what did he do?
    Telemachus was the son of Odysseus and Penelope. He finally went in search of his father.

6. How did the Phaeacians help Odysseus?
    After Odysseus related his story to King Alcinous, the king gave him a ship. The other men gave him presents and provisions.

7. What happened to Odysseus and his men when they reached Circe's island?
    Circe turned the men into swine. Hermes helped Odysseus resist her powers, and she was so impressed that she released his men and treated them as her guests.

8. Where did Odysseus have to go to find out how to get home?
    He had to travel to Hades, find the spirit of the prophet Teiresias, and then follow his directions.

9. How did Odysseus get rid of the suitors when he arrived home?
    Athena disguised him as a beggar. He was able to make himself known to his son, Telemachus, and Eumaeus, a servant. Penelope had proposed that whomever could shoot Odysseus's bow would be her next husband. (She didn't know the beggar was Odysseus.)

Telemachus gave the bow to Odysseus. He began shooting all of the suitors. Telemachus and Eumaeus joined in, and murdered all of the men.

10. What is the source for the adventures of Aeneas?
    It is the *Aeneid*, the greatest of Latin poems, by Virgil.

11. Why did Aeneas go on a journey?
    He had escaped when the Greeks defeated Troy. He was looking for a new place to live. He eventually ended up in Italy, and was believed to be the real founder of Rome.

12. Who was Dido, and why was she important?
    She was the founder and ruler of Carthage. Aeneas landed there. Cupid made her fall in love with Aeneas.

13. What role did Juno and Venus have in the story of Aeneas?
    Juno wanted to stop him because she hated the Trojans. Venus liked them, and helped Aeneas.

14. Where did Aeneas go when he left Carthage?
    He went to see the Sibyl of Cumae, who told him to search for the golden bough. He then went to the lower world to see his father and get further instructions.

15. Briefly describe the war in Italy.
    Aeneas wanted to marry Lavinia, the daughter of Latium. (This had been prophesied.) Hera convinced one of the Furies to start a war between Aeneas and Turnus, King of the Rutulians, and another suitor of Lavinia. Eventually Aeneas killed Turnus, won the war, and married Lavinia. They became the founders of the Roman race.

Part Five *The Great Families of Mythology*
Chapter 17 *The House of Atreus* Chapter 18 *The House of Thebes*
Chapter 19 *The Royal House of Athens*

1. Name two of the members of the house of Atreus.
    Agamemnon, the Greek hero in the Trojan War, was the son of Atreus. Agamemnon's wife was Clytemnestra, and his children were Iphigenia, Orestes, and Electra. Menelaus was his brother, and husband of Helen.

2. Who brought all of the misfortunes on the house of Atreus?
    It was Tantalus, a King of Lydia.

3. What was the evil deed Tantalus committed?
    Tantalus had his son killed and boiled, and he served this dish to the gods at a banquet.

4. What punishment did Tantalus receive for this deed?
    He was placed in a pool in Hades. Whenever he stooped to drink, the water drained away. When he reached above to pick fruit from the tree, the wind tossed the fruit out of his reach.

5. What did Tantalus's daughter, Niobe, do, and how was she punished?
    She ordered the people of Thebes to worship her as a goddess. Apollo and Artemis were angered, and they shot all of Niobe's children as she watched. Then they changed her into a stone.

6. Why had Agamemnon killed his daughter Iphigenia?
    The Greek army had needed strong winds to sail to Troy. They convinced Agamemnon that if he sacrificed his daughter, the winds would turn in their favor.

7. How did Agamemnon die?
    His wife, Clytemnestra, killed him. She had never forgiven him for sacrificing their daughter.

8. What happened to Clytemnestra and her lover, Aegisthus?
    They were killed by her son, Orestes.

9. What one good thing resulted from Orestes' repentance?
    The gods established a new law of mercy. They acquitted Orestes and ended the curse.

10. What did Cadmus do?
    He founded the city of Thebes.

11. What happened to Cadmus and Harmonia, and what did this show?
    They were turned into serpents. This showed that suffering was not always a punishment for evil, but that the innocent could also suffer.

12. What wrongs did Oedipus commit?
    He killed his father, King Laius, and married his mother, Jocasta.

13. Did he commit this crime knowingly?
    No. He thought he was the son of King Polybus. He had left that land because of the prophecy that he would kill his father.

14. What punishment did Oedipus inflict upon himself?
    He blinded himself.

15. Why was Antigone killed?
    She defied Creon's orders and buried her dead brother, Polyneices.

16. How did Theseus, King of Athens, help Adrastus and the relatives of the chieftains who fought against Thebes?
    He took his army into Thebes and forced Creon to allow the dead chieftains a proper burial.

17. For what was Cecrops noted?
    He was responsible for Athena becoming the protector of Athens.

18. How did Philomela let Procne know of Tereus' evil deeds?
    She wove the story into a tapestry and had the tapestry delivered to Procne.

19. What happened to Procne and Philomela?
    The gods changed them into birds. Procne became a nightingale. Philomela became a swallow. Since Philomela didn't have a tongue, the swallow could only twitter, not sing.

20. How did Cephalus test Procris's devotion to him?
    He disguised himself and tried to make her fall in love with the stranger.

21. How were Cerusa and Ion reunited?
    Cerusa went to the oracle at Delphi to find out what had happened to her son. While there she discovered that the young lad who attended the oracle was her son.

Part Six *The Less Important Myths*
Chapter 20 *Midas and Others*   Chapter 21 *Brief Myths*

1. What wish did Bacchus grant to Midas, and what was the result?
    He wished that everything he touched would turn to gold. When he tried to eat, and his meal turned to gold, he realized the folly of his wish. He asked Bacchus to take the favor back, which he did.

2. For what was Aesculapius honored?
    People believed he healed the sick.

3. What wrong did the Danaids do, and what was their punishment?
   They killed their husbands on their collective wedding night. They were sent to the underworld, where they had to try to carry water in jars filled with holes. They were forced to repeat this futile task time and time again.

4. What was Arachne's misdeed, and what was her punishment?
   Arachne was a weaver who declared that her work was as good as Minerva's. Minerva challenged her to a contest. When it appeared that the girl's work was as good as the goddess's, Minerva beat her. Arachne hanged herself, but Minerva revived the body and turned Arachne into a spider.

5. Which human lover of Zeus' was changed into the Great Bear and placed in the sky?
   This was Callisto.

6. For what was the Centaur Chiron known?
   He was kind and wise. He trained many of the sons of heroes, including Achilles.

7. Who were the Myrmidons?
   They were men created from ants on the island of Aegina. Zeus created them in answer to a prayer by Aeacus, the king.

8. Which great hunter was placed in the sky as a constellation?
   It was Orion.

9. Who were the Pleiades?
   They were the seven daughters of Atlas. Orion pursued them. Zeus rescued them by placing them in the sky.

10. What did Sisyphus do, and how was he punished?
    He told the river god that Zeus had carried away the god's daughter. Zeus punished him by sending him to Hades and making him roll a rock uphill. The rock continually rolled back downhill.

Part 7 *The Mythology of the Norsemen*
Introduction   Chapter 22 *The Stories of Signy and Sigurd*   Chapter 23 *The Norse Gods*

1. What was Asgard like?
   The home of the gods was grave and solemn, with a threat of doom always present.

2. What was the Norse outlook on good and evil?
   They believed that evil would eventually triumph. Nevertheless, they continued to fight for the good.

3. What was the choice the Norse hero made?
   The Norse hero chose between yielding to evil or dying for good.

4. What was the central theme of the Norse mythology?
   Victory was possible in death, and courage was never defeated.

5. What was the central theme of the Norse mythology?
   Victory was possible in death, and courage was never defeated.

6. Briefly retell the story of Signy and Sigmund.
   They were brother and sister. Signy's husband killed her father and all of her brothers except Sigurd. She disguised herself, visited him, and conceived a son, Sinfiotli. She later sent the boy to live with Sigmund. Sigmund and Sinfiotli killed Signy's husband and children in retaliation. Then she killed herself.

7. Whom did Sigurd rescue?
   He rescued Brynhild, a Valkyrie, from a ring of fire.

8. How did Sigurd die?
   Gunnar convinced his brother to kill Sigurd while he was sleeping.

9. How did Balder die?
   Loki persuaded Balder's blind brother, Hoder, to throw a twig of mistletoe at Balder. The poisonous twig pierced Balder's heart and killed him.

10. Describe Odin and his duties.
    He was aloof and solemn. He was always searching for more wisdom. He was responsible for postponing the day of doom. He often suffered in order to receive more knowledge.

11. Who were the Valkyries?
    The name means "Choosers of the Slain." They waited on the tables of the gods in Asgard. They also went to the battlefield with Odin and decided who would live and die. They carried the dead to Valhalla, the Hall of the Slain.

12. Which days of the week were named after Norse gods?
    Thursday was named for Thor, the Thunder God. Wednesday was named for Odin, which was Woden in the south. Tuesday was named for Tyr, the God of War, and Friday was named for Freya, the Goddess of Love and Beauty.

13. Who ruled the Kingdom of Death?
    It was ruled by Hela, and was called Niflheim.

14. How did Odin and his brothers make the world?
    They killed their father, the Giant Ymir. They made the earth from his body and the heavens from his skull. They used his blood for the sea.

15. Who was the Thunder-God?
    It was Thor.

16. Who was Odin's wife?
    It was Frigga.

17. Who was Tyr?
    He was the God of War.

18. Who was the goddess of Love and Beauty?
    It was Freya.

19. What was Midgard?
    It was the battlefield for men. Women were not admitted.

20. What did the Norsemen believe would happen after Odin and the other gods were defeated by evil?
    They believed that another would come who would triumph over evil.

21. What, according to Hamilton, were the Norsemen's two characteristics?
    They were heroic and had common sense.

MULTIPLE CHOICE STUDY GUIDE QUESTIONS - *Mythology*

<u>Introduction</u>

1. True or False: The myths have elements of science, literature, and religion.
    A. True
    B. False

2. What is the first written record of Greece called, and who was the author?
    A. It is the *Apuleid*, written by Ovid.
    B. It is the *Opus Colossus*, written by Hesiod.
    C. It is the *Iliad*, written by Homer.
    D. It is the *Pausanias*, written by Catullus.

3. True or False: The myths show us how much the early Greeks had progressed from primitive man.
    A. True
    B. False

4. What happened to the portrayal of Zeus over the years?
    A. He became more of a tyrant and omnipotent ruler.
    B. He became the common father and guardian of mankind.
    C. He became less important as the other gods became more important.
    D. He became more and more perfect until mankind gave up hope of ever imitating him.

5. What is the name of one account of the creation of the universe and the gods that is important to mythology?
    A. It is the *Theogony*.
    B. It is the *Homeric Hymn*.
    C. It is the *Titanuis*.
    D. It is the *Mythos Hesperius*.

Multiple Choice Study Guide Questions - *Mythology*

Part One *The Gods, The Creation, and The Earliest Heroes*
Chapter 1 *The Gods* Chapter 2 *The Two Great Gods of Earth*

1. What did the Greeks believe about the origins of the gods and the universe?
    A. They believed that the gods created the universe.
    B. They believed that a being who was supreme even over the gods created the gods and the universe.
    C. They believed that the universe and the gods were never really created; they always were.
    D. The Greeks believed that the universe created the gods.

2. Who were the first parents?
    A. Heaven and Earth were the first parents.
    B. The Titans were the first parents.
    C. The gods were the first parents.
    D. Night and Day were the first parents.

3. True or False: Homer described Olympus as heaven.
    A. True
    B. False

4. Which of the following gives the correct Greek and Roman equivalents for the names of the gods and goddesses?
    A. Zeus = Saturn; Hades = Hela; Artemis = Venus; Hermes = Vulcan.
    B. Zeus = Cronus; Hades = Pluto; Artemis = Ares; Hermes = Mars.
    C. Zeus = Jupiter; Hades = Pluto; Artemis = Diana; Hermes = Mercury.
    D. Zeus= Hyperion; Hades = Neptune; Artemis = Minerva; Hermes = Vesta.

5. Which is the only god whose name is the same in both Greek and Roman mythology?
    A. It is Poseidon.
    B. It is Venus.
    C. It is Phoebus Apollo.
    D. It is Pallas Athena.

6. How was the will of Zeus revealed at the oracle at Dodona?
    A. The priestess read messages in the bumps on the bark of the oak trees.
    B. The priests interpreted the messages in the thunder and lightning that were ever present over the area.
    C. The priestess went into a trance and then spoke through the voice of Zeus.
    D. The priests interpreted the rustling of the oak leaves.

Multiple Choice Study Guide Questions - *Mythology*

Part 1 Chapters 1 & 2 continued

7. Whose symbols are being described? The breastplate was the aegis, the bird was the eagle, and the oak was the tree.
    A. These belonged to Zeus.
    B. These belonged to Poseidon.
    C. These belonged to Hades.
    D. These belonged to Apollo.

8. What was the relationship between Zeus and Hera?
    A. She was only his wife.
    B. She was both his mother and his wife.
    C. She was only his daughter.
    D. She was both his wife and sister.

9. True or False: Hera was the protector of marriage. She was usually portrayed as loving and kind, and very supportive of the many mortal females with whom Zeus fell in love.
    A True
    B. False

10. Who were Zeus's two brothers, and where did they rule?
    A. Hades ruled the underworld and Hephaestus ruled the sea.
    B. Oceanus ruled the sea and Poseidon ruled the underworld.
    C. Poseidon ruled the sea and Hades ruled the underworld.
    D. Poseidon ruled the sea and Thanatos ruled the underworld.

11. Which of the following statements is **not** correct?
    A. Athena was known as the "goddess with three forms:" Selene in the sky, Athena on earth and Hecate in the underworld.
    B. Phoebus Apollo played the golden lyre, and was also the Archer and Healer. His oracle at Delphi was a direct link between gods and men.
    C. Artemis was the Huntsman in Chief and the protector of youth and wildlife.
    D. Aphrodite was the Goddess of Love and Beauty.

12. Who is being described? He was the God of Fire. He made the armor and furniture for the gods. He was also the patron of handicrafts and the protector of smiths.
    A. It was Ares.
    B. It was Lucifus.
    C. It was Hestia.
    D. It was Hephaestus.

Multiple Choice Study Guide Questions - *Mythology*

Part One   Chapters 1 & 2 continued

13. True or False: Hermes was the messenger of the gods. He had winged sandals on his feet, wings on hat and magic wand.
    A. True
    B. False

14. Which sea god was able to foretell the future and change his shape at will?
    A. Triton
    B. Ocean
    C. Nereus
    D. Proteus

15. Who ferried the souls of the dead across the water to the underworld?
    A. Persephone
    B. Charon
    C. Cerberus
    D. The Furies

16. What were the Elysian Fields?
    A. They were the place of torment where the evil was punished.
    B. They were along the banks of the River Styx. The dead waited there until they were sent to reward or punishment.
    C. They were the place of blessedness where the good were rewarded.
    D. They were a special section of the underworld where children who died were sent.

17. Whose story is told here? She was the Goddess of the Corn. Her daughter was carried off to the underworld by Hades. The mother was greatly upset, and no crops grew on the earth. Zeus then ruled that the daughter would spend four months of every year in the underworld, and the rest of the time on the earth with her mother. The crops grew and flowers bloomed while the daughter was on earth, but all died when she went to the underworld.
    A. Demeter was the mother and Persephone was the daughter.
    B. Ceres was the mother and Phoebe was the daughter.
    C. Persephone was the mother and Doria was the daughter.
    D. Rhea was the mother and Demeter was the daughter.

18. True or False: Dionysus was the God of the Vine. He could give either joy or savage brutality, because wine could be both bad and good.
    A. True
    B. False

Multiple Choice Study Guide Questions - *Mythology*

Part One Chapters 1 & 2 continued

19. Who became the center of the belief in immortality?
    A. It was Demeter.
    B. It was Persephone.
    C. It was Dionysus.
    D. It was Hades.

20. How were Demeter and Dionysus different from the other gods and goddesses?
    A. They were the only ones who had human mothers.
    B. They were the only ones who did not have temples dedicated to them.
    C. They were the only ones to whom humans could speak directly.
    D. They were the only ones who knew suffering, as the mortals did.

Multiple Choice Study Guide Questions - *Mythology*

Part One *The Gods, The Creation, and The Earliest Heroes*
Chapter 3 *How the World and Mankind Were Created*   Chapter 4 *The Earliest Heroes*

1. What did the Greeks think was at the very beginning of things?
    A. They thought Cosmos, or a mix of everything, was at the beginning.
    B. They thought it was Water, the gift of Life.
    C. They thought it was Eternity.
    D. They thought Chaos, or formless confusion, was at the beginning.

2. What did Love create?
    A. Night and the Stars
    B. Erebus
    C. Light and Day
    D. Earth

3. Which of the following does not describe Cronus?
    A. Cronus was a Giant.
    B. He wounded his father, Heaven, because his mother, Earth, asked him to.
    C. He became Lord of the Universe and ruled with his sister, Rhea.
    D. Cronus ate five of his six children because he knew that one of them would one day dethrone him.

4. True or False: Zeus became the ruler of heaven and earth when he mastered the use of thunder and lightning, and his brothers and sisters helped him defeat Cronus.
    A. True
    B. False

5. True or False: The Greeks thought the Earth was a round disk. The Sea flowed around the earth. The Land of the Dead was under the Earth.
    A. True
    B. False

6. What did Prometheus give men to protect them?
    A. He gave men the gift of language.
    B. He gave men the gift of reason.
    C. He gave men the gift of love.
    D. He gave men the gift of fire.

Multiple Choice Study Guide Questions - *Mythology*
Part One   Chapters 3 & 4 continued

7. Which of the following does **not** describe Pandora?
    A. Zeus intended for her and all women to be beautiful, but an evil to men.
    B. She was the first woman, and was lovely.
    C. Her name means "Full of Evil and Sorrow."
    D. Zeus created her to punish mankind for tricking him into accepting the fat and bones of any sacrificial animals.

8. True or False: The gods gave Pandora a box and told her to collect all of the evils in world. They said if she did this, that men would be pleased with her.
    A. True
    B. False

9. How did Zeus punish Prometheus?
    A. Prometheus was sent to a very small island. He could only stand up and crouch down because it was so small. He never got any rest.
    B. Prometheus had to stand in a place between Night and Day and hold the world on his back forever.
    C. Prometheus was bound to a rock. Every day an eagle would come down and eat Prometheus' liver.
    D. Prometheus was forced to feel the hurt and sorrow of every human being. He was in constant pain for all eternity.

10. Who is being described? She was a maiden with whom Zeus fell in love. He turned her into a calf to fool Hera, and was forced to leave her that way. Eventually she was returned to human form. Hercules was her direct descendent.
    A. Io
    B. Epimetheus
    C. Pyrrha
    D. Deucalion

11. How did Zeus carry off Europa?
    A. He sent the Sun in his golden chariot to kidnap her.
    B. He changed into a baby. When she bent to pick him up, he changed back and took her away.
    C. He had the North Wind blow her to the island of Crete.
    D. He changed into a bull and carried her away from her home.

Multiple Choice Study Guide Questions - *Mythology*
Part One Chapters 3 & 4 continued

12.-15. Matching. Match the following descriptions with the characters being described. Answer choices are given below the descriptions.

12. He was the Cyclops whom Odysseus encountered on his way home from the Trojan War.

13. He was a beautiful lad who refused to fall in love with any maiden. The goddess Nemesis made him fall in love with his reflection in a pool. He would not look away from his reflection, and so he died. A lovely flower bloomed on the spot where he died, and it was named after him.

14. She was a nymph. Hera punished her unjustly by condemning her to only be able to repeat what was said. She was in love with Narcissus, but was not able to tell him so. She wasted away and only her voice was left.

15. Aphrodite and Persephone were both in love with him. Zeus declared that he should spend half of the year with each of them. One day while he was hunting, he was gored by a boar and died. The red flowers called anemones bloomed on his drops of blood.

    A. Narcissus
    B. Adonis
    C. Echo
    D. Polyphemus

Multiple Choice Study Guide Questions - *Mythology*

Part Two *Stories of Love and Adventure*
Chapter 5 *Cupid and Psyche*   Chapter 6 *Eight Brief Tales of Lovers*

1. Why was Venus angry at Psyche?
    A. Psyche tried to attract Zeus' attention because she wanted to have a child who would be partly a god. This angered Hera, who asked Venus to help her punish Psyche.
    B. Psyche was the loveliest maiden alive. Many mortals began worshipping her and forgot Venus. This angered the goddess and she planned to punish Psyche.
    C. Psyche had wrongly fallen in love with her father. This was always frowned upon by the gods, and Venus wanted to stop her.
    D. Psyche believed that mortals should be free to choose their own lovers, instead of having Venus or Cupid choose for them. She convinced many people who began defying the choices of Venus and Cupid.

2. Was Venus' plan for revenge successful?
    A. Yes, it was.
    B. No, it wasn't.

3. True or False: Psyche discovered that Cupid was her husband. He fled from her when she saw him. She had betrayed his trust by looking at him after she had promised not to.
    A. True
    B. False

4. True or False: Cupid and Psyche were finally married in Olympus. Zeus made Psyche a goddess. Love and the Soul were together forever.
    A. True
    B. False

5. Which lovers arranged a tryst, mistakenly thought the other had been killed, and killed themselves?
    A. Galatea and Alpheus
    B. Zephyr and Amalina
    C. Pyramus and Thisbe
    D. Phoebe and Creos

Multiple Choice Study Guide Questions - *Mythology*
Part Two Chapters 5 & 6   continued

6. What happened to Pygmalion?
   A. The moon fell in love with him and put him into a magic slumber.
   B. He chased Arethusa until Artemis turned her into a spring of water.
   C. He killed the woman he loved in a jealous rage because she loved another. The gods punished him by making sure no woman ever fell in love with him again.
   D. He fell in love with a statue that he had made. Venus brought the statue to life and they married.

7-10 Matching. Match the following descriptions with the characters being described. Answer choices are given below the descriptions.

7. He was the son of one of the Muses, and a gifted musician. He was irresistible when he played and sang. He wooed a maiden, but she died on their wedding day. He went to the underworld and tried to bring her back. Hades agreed, as long as he did not turn around to look at her before they were out of the underworld. When he was back in the upper world, he thought she was, too, and he turned to look at her. She was still in the cavern of the underworld, and she was taken back to the underworld.

8. He was the son of Lucifer, the light bearer. His wife was the daughter of the King of the Winds. The two were never apart. He was killed at sea, but she was unaware and waited for him at home. Morpheus finally appeared to her in her husband's form and told her that her husband was dead. The next morning she found her husband's body in the water. Then she and her dead husband were turned into birds.

9. This poor married couple gave hospitality to Jupiter and Mercury when they came to earth in disguise. The gods offered them a reward, but all they asked was to become priests of the temple that Jupiter and Mercury created. They asked the gods to let them die together. The gods changed them into a linden and an oak tree that grew from the same trunk.

10. Apollo fell in love with this daughter of the river god. She did not love Apollo or any mortal man. She only wanted to be a huntress, like Diana. Apollo began chasing her, and she cried to her father for help. To protect her, her father turned her into a laurel tree.
    A. Ceyx and Alcyone
    B. Peneus and Daphne
    C. Orpheus and Eurydice
    D. Baucis and Philemon

Multiple Choice Study Guide Questions - *Mythology*

Part Two *Stories of Love and Adventure*
Chapter 7 *The Quest of the Golden Fleece*   Chapter 8 *Four Great Adventures*

1. Why was Jason's journey significant?
    A. It was the first journey ever made over land instead of water.
    B. It was the first journey that was ever recorded.
    C. Jason made the first map while on his journey.
    D. Jason was the first hero in Europe who went on a great journey.

2. True or False: Hermes had given the Golden Fleece to Phrixus to wear as a coat. King Aeetes in stole it from him.
    A. True
    B. False

3. Why did Jason undertake the search for the Golden Fleece?
    A. Jason was trying to regain the kingdom that had been taken from his father by a cousin. The cousin agreed to give it back if Jason could bring him the Golden Fleece.
    B. Jason had heard that the Fleece had wonderful healing powers. He wanted to get it and cure his sick parents.
    C. Jason wanted to prove that he was as great as one of the gods. He thought if he got t the Golden Fleece and gave it to the gods, that they would reward him with immortality.
    D. The Golden Fleece was worth a lot of money. Jason wanted to get it and sell it. He wanted to buy a fleet of ships and begin trade with other countries.

4. What were the harpies?
    A. They were beautiful maidens who played harps. Men who heard their music went insane.
    B. They were fierce warriors with huge harpoons. The harpoons never missed their target. Men were afraid to sail past the island where the Harpies lived.
    C. The Harpies were flying creatures with sharp claws and hooked beaks. They left behind a terrible smell.
    D. They were sea creatures that were part harp seal and part man. They overturned ships and ate the drowning sailors.

5. True or False: The sons of the North Wind, who were traveling with Jason, killed the Harpies.
    A. True
    B. False

Multiple Choice Study Guide Questions - *Mythology*
Part Two Chapters 7 & 8 continued

6. What was the name of Jason's ship?
   A. His ship was the *Argo*.
   B. His ship was the *Rhodes*.
   C. His ship was the *Arethusa*.
   D. His ship was the *Hellespont*.

7. Which of the following was not one of the heroes who traveled with Jason?
   A. Hercules
   B. Castor
   C. Achilles
   D. Orpheus

8. Who were the warrior-daughters of Harmony and Ares?
   A. The Caucasus
   B. The Amazons
   C. The Hypsiplyes
   D. The Symplegades

9. Which of the following was **not** a part of the task that Jason performed for King Aeetes in order to get the Golden Fleece?
   A. Jason yoked two fierce bulls together and used them to plow a field.
   B. He killed a dragon and pulled its teeth.
   C. He sowed the dragon's teeth in the field.
   D. He killed the armed warriors who sprang up from the dragon's teeth.

10. Who helped Jason, and why?
    A. Medea gave him charms to use. She did this because Cupid had made her fall in love with Jason.
    B. Colchus did, because he wanted revenge for mistreatment from the king.
    C. Apsyrtus, the son of King Aeetes, did. He wanted the kingdom for himself.
    D. Athena disguised herself as a sailor and told Jason how to defeat King Aeetes.

11. What did Phaethon want to do?
    A. He wanted to walk from one end of the earth to the other.
    B. He wanted to hide on Mount Olympus and spy on the gods.
    C. He wanted to drive the Sun's chariot for a day.
    D. He wanted to set the world on fire and destroy it.

Multiple Choice Study Guide Questions - *Mythology*
Part Two Chapters 7 & 8 continued

12. Who were Pegasus and Bellerophon?
    A. They were the two sons of Hades who were allowed to stay on earth as long as they performed good deeds.
    B. Bellerophon was a son of Poseidon and a mortal woman. Pegasus was a winged horse.
    C. They were two of the warriors who went on the journey with Jason.
    D. They were the first dogs. They lived in the stables on Olympus and were also known as "The Hounds of Zeus."

13. What monster did Pegasus and Bellerophon destroy?
    A. They destroyed the Giant, Aloadae.
    B. They destroyed the Chimaera, which was part lion, serpent, and goat.
    C. They destroyed the two-headed Hippocrene.
    D. They destroyed the evil Proteus. Proteus could change to any shape at will.

14. Which father and son used wings made by the father to escape from the Labyrinth?
    A. Ovid was the father, and Apollodorus was the son.
    B. Ephialtes was the father, and Dodonus was the son.
    C. Otus was the father, and Polydus was the son.
    D. Daedalus was the father, and Icarus was the son.

15. True or False: The son flew too close to the sun and the glue on the wings melted. He fell into the sea. The father escaped to Sicily.
    A. True
    B. False

Multiple Choice Study Guide Questions - *Mythology*

Part Three *The Great Heroes Before the Trojan War*
Chapter 9 *Perseus*   Chapter 10 *Theseus*   Chapter 11 *Hercules*   Chapter 12 *Atalanta*

1. What was the Medusa?
    A. She was a one-eyed monster that could read minds and make a person insane.
    B. She was nymph with a sweet voice. Anyone who heard her sing would forget everything and live only to hear the singing.
    C. She was a Gorgon, with hair made of snakes. Anyone who looked at her would turn to stone.
    D. She was part woman and part lion. She guarded the overland passage into Greece. No one could travel on that route because she killed all who tried.

2. True or False: Perseus used Hermes' sword and Athena's shield. He looked into the shield at Medusa's reflection and cut off her head.
    A. True
    B. False

3. How did Perseus kill his grandfather?
    A. He held up Medusa's head and the man died when he looked at it.
    B. He killed his grandfather in a sword fight.
    C. He threw a discus that swerved and accidentally killed his grandfather.
    D. His grandfather was so shocked to find him alive that he died of a stroke.

4. True or False: Theseus had a scar from a knife wound that his father had made. This was the way that his father recognized Theseus as his son when he went to Athens.
    A. True
    B. False

5. Which creature is being described: It was half bull, half human, the son of King Minos of Crete. It lived in the Labyrinth made by Daedalus. Every nine years fourteen young Athenians were sacrificed to it.
    A. It was the Hippolytus.
    B. It was the Minotaur.
    C. It was the Sphinx.
    D. It was the Pasiphae.

Multiple Choice Study Guide Questions - *Mythology*
Part Three   Chapters 9, 10, 11, & 12 continued

6. How did Theseus find his way out of the Labyrinth?
   A. The King's daughter, Ariadne, gave him a ball of thread which he unwound as he went through the Labyrinth. He killed the beast and followed the string out.
   B. He had put marks along the wall with an invisible paint that Athena had given him. Only he could see it. He followed the marks back after he killed the beast.
   C. Daedalus had secretly given Theseus a copy of the design plan for the Labyrinth. Theseus marked his route on this and followed it out.
   D. Hera made a beam of sunlight shine along the path he was to take to get out.

7. How did Theseus change the government of Athens?
   A. He established a monarchy with a line of succession that could only come from his descendants.
   B. He established the first aristocracy.
   C. He developed the first Code of Justice by which all men were to live.
   D. He organized a commonwealth and let the people govern themselves.

8. True or False: Theseus' son, Hippolytus, fell in love with Theseus' second wife, Phaedra. When Phaedra would not return his love, he killed her.
   A. True
   B. False

9. What was Hercules' main characteristic?
   A. He was the smartest man on earth.
   B. He was the strongest man on earth.
   C. He was the bravest man on earth.
   D. He was the fastest man on earth.

10. Why did Hercules perform his twelve labors?
    A. He was doing penance for killing his wife and children.
    B. Theseus challenged him to see who the greatest hero in Greece was.
    C. Zeus had told Hercules that if he could perform all of the labors successfully, he would be given immortality and a place among the gods.
    D. He had to do them before he could marry the woman he loved.

Multiple Choice Study Guide Questions - *Mythology*
Part Three Chapters 9, 10, 11, & 12 continued

11. Which of the following was not one of the labors of Hercules?
    A. He killed the lion of Nemea by choking it.
    B. He killed the nine-headed Hydra.
    C. He brought back alive a stag with golden horns.
    D. He captured a ferocious dragon.

12. How did Hercules clean the Augean stables?
    A. He caused a powerful wind that blew the dirt away.
    B. He picked them up and shook the filth out.
    C. He diverted two rivers and made them flood the stables.
    D. He made a huge plow, attached it to the horses, and plowed the dirt out.

13. True or False: Hercules kidnapped the Queen of the Amazons and married her.
    A. True
    B. False

14. Which of the following was not one of the labors of Hercules?
    A. He brought back the cattle of Geryon.
    B. He brought back the Golden Apples of the Hesperides.
    C. He went to the underworld and freed Theseus from the Chair of Forgetfulness.
    D. He captured two giants and forced them to hold up the world so that Atlas could be freed from his burden.

15. Whom did Atalanta tell her father she would marry?
    A. She said she would marry the man who could swim further out into the sea than she could.
    B. She said she would marry the man who could shoot an arrow further than she could.
    C. She said she would marry the man who could beat her in a foot race.
    D. She said she would marry the man who could defeat her at arm wrestling.

Multiple Choice Study Guide Questions - *Mythology*

Part Four *The Heroes of the Trojan War*
Chapter 13 *The Trojan War*   Chapter 14 *The Fall of Troy*

1. True or False: Hamilton took most of the story of the Trojan War from Homer's *Odyssey*.
    A. True
    B. False

2. Which of the following does **not** describe the Judgment of Paris?
    A. Hestia, Aphrodite, and Artemis were feuding over who was the fairest.
    B. The winner's prize was a golden apple.
    C. Paris was asked to listen to each of the bribes and choose who would get the prize.
    D. Paris awarded the prize to Aphrodite.

3. True or False: The Trojan War started because Paris kidnapped Helen, the Greek wife of King Menelaus of Sparta. Helen's former suitors allied with Menelaus to get her back.
    A. True
    B. False

4. Who was **not** a main combatant on the Greek side?
    A. Odysseus
    B. Achilles
    C. Priam
    D. Agamemnon

5. Which gods favored the Trojan side?
    A. Hera, Zeus, and Hephaestus favored the Trojans.
    B. Artemis, Poseidon, Athena, and Hades favored the Trojans.
    C. Aphrodite, Ares, Apollo, and Artemis favored the Trojans.
    D. Ares and Hestia favored the Trojans.

6. Who was killed during the battle between Achilles and Hector?
    A. Achilles was killed.
    B. Hector was killed.

7. True or False: Paris shot an arrow at Achilles. Apollo guided the arrow to Achilles' right shoulder which was his only vulnerable spot.
    A. True
    B. False

Multiple Choice Study Guide Questions - *Mythology*
Part Four Chapters 13 & 14 continued

8. What did Diomedes steal from the city of Troy?
    A. He stole the sacred image of Pallas Athena.
    B. He stole the book of military maneuvers.
    C. He stole the keys to the gates of Troy.
    D. He stole the battle flags.

9. True or False: The Greeks dug a tunnel under the wall into the temple and entered the city.
    A. True
    B. False

10. Which of the Trojans escaped, and who helped them?
    A. Aphrodite helped Aeneas, his father, and his son to escape.
    B. Artemis helped Priam and his wife to escape.
    C. Apollo helped Hecuba and Andromache to escape.
    D. Zeus helped Astanyax, his mother, and Polyxena to escape.

Multiple Choice Study Guide Questions - *Mythology*

Part Four *The Heroes of the Trojan War*
Chapter 15 *The Adventures of Odysseus*   Chapter 16 *The Adventures of Aeneas*

1. From which mythology source did Edith Hamilton take the adventures of Odysseus?
    A. The *Iliad*
    B. The *Theogeny*
    C. The *Odyssey*
    D. The *Homeric Edda*

2. What caused Athena to become angry at the Greeks?
    A. The Greeks found a prophetess, Cassandra, in Athena's temple in Troy. They dragged her out. Athena was angry at the sacrilege.
    B. The Greeks gave Hera the credit for their victory, although it was really Athena who helped them. Athena was jealous.
    C. The Greeks only offered Athena a meager gift as a thanks for her help, and she thought she deserved more.
    D. The Greeks took all of the credit of victory themselves, and said they did not need the help of the gods.

3. How did Poseidon avenge Athena?
    A. He changed most of the Greek warriors into fish. He spared Odysseus because she asked him to.
    B. He calmed the waters so the ships could not sail. Many of the men died of thirst.
    C. He sent a pod of whales to push the Greek ships so far off course that most of them never found their way home again.
    D. He caused a great tempest in the sea. The Greek fleet was scattered, and many men drowned. Odysseus remained alive, but was shipwrecked.

4. True or False: Penelope had given up hope of ever seeing Odysseus again, and had agreed to marry one of the suitors.
    A. True
    B. False

5. Who was the son of Odysseus and Penelope who went in search of his father?
    A. It was Menelaus.
    B. It was Nestor.
    C. It was Telemachus.
    D. It was Mentor.

Multiple Choice Study Guide Questions - *Mythology*
Part Four Chapters 15 & 16 continued

6. How did the Phaeacians help Odysseus?
    A. They gave him a map and a guide.
    B. They gave him a ship and provisions.
    C. They prayed for him.
    D. They guided him all the way home.

7. Who turned the men into swine, then released them and treated them as her guests?
    A. It was Circe.
    B. It was Helen.
    C. It was Nausicaa.
    D. It was Ino.

8. True or False: In order to get home, Odysseus first had to travel to Hades, find the spirit of the prophet Teiresias, and then follow his directions.
    A. True
    B. False

9. Which of the following did **not** happen when Odysseus arrived home?
    A. Athena disguised Odysseus as a beggar.
    B. His real identity remained a secret from everyone until the end.
    C. Penelope had proposed that whomever could shoot Odysseus' bow would be her next husband.
    D. Odysseus took the bow and began shooting the suitors.

10. Name the source and the author for the adventures of Aeneas.
    A. It is *The Adventurous Aeneas* by Hesperious.
    B. It is *The Pax Augusta* by Ulysses.
    C. It is *The Theogony* by Hesoid.
    D. It is *The Aeneid* by Virgil.

11. Why did Aeneas go on a journey?
    A. He blamed himself for losing the Trojan War, and wanted to repent his wrongs.
    B. He wanted to prove that a Trojan could have as many daring adventures as a Greek.
    C. He was looking for a new place to live after the Greeks destroyed Troy.
    D. He was looking for the underworld. He wanted to end his life because he was so upset about losing the war.

Multiple Choice Study Guide Questions - *Mythology*
Part Four Chapters 15 & 16 continued

12. Which of the following does **not** describe Dido?
    A. She was the founder and ruler of Carthage.
    B. Cupid made her fall in love with Aeneas.
    C. She married Aeneas and made him the King of Carthage.
    D. She killed herself when Aeneas left her.

13. True or False: Juno wanted to stop Aeneas because she hated the Trojans. Venus liked them, and helped Aeneas.
    A. True
    B. False

14. Where did Aeneas go when he left Carthage?
    A. He went to the Oracle at Delphi to get advice.
    B. He went to find the golden apple of knowledge.
    C. He went to Ethiopia to pay homage to Neptune and ask for a safe journey.
    D. He went to the lower world to see his father and get further instructions.

15. Which did **not** happen as a result of the war in Italy?
    A. Aeneas killed Turnus.
    B. Aeneas and Lavinia became the first Italians.
    C. Aeneas married Lavinia.
    D. All of the enemies of Aeneas were destroyed.

Multiple Choice Study Guide Questions - *Mythology*

Part Five *The Great Families of Mythology*
Chapter 17 *The House of Atreus*   Chapter 18 *The House of Thebes*
Chapter 19 *The Royal House of Athens*

1. Which of the following was not a member of the house of Atreus?
    A. Agamemnon
    B. Electra
    C. Menelaus
    D. Eumenides

2. What was the evil deed that Tantalus committed?
    A. He killed his father and married his sister.
    B. He said there were no gods, and forbade his subjects to worship them.
    C. He had his son killed and boiled, and he served this dish to the gods at a banquet.
    D. He tried to kidnap Aphrodite and keep her as his lover.

3. True or False: As a punishment, Tantalus was placed in a pool in Hades. Whenever he stooped to drink, the water drained away. When he reached above to pick fruit from the tree, the wind tossed the fruit out of his reach.

    A. True
    B. False

4. What did Tantalus' daughter, Niobe, do, and how was she punished?
    A. She defied the gods and tried to rescue her father. She was given the same punishment as he was.
    B. She ordered the people of Thebes to worship her as a goddess. Apollo and Artemis were angered, and they shot all of Niobe's children as she watched. Then they changed her into a stone.
    C. She broke a branch from a tree that was the home of a dryad. Instead of trying to heal the tree and save the dryad, she left them to die. The dryad changed her into a tree.
    D. She killed the child that she had by Zeus, and told him it was born dead. When he discovered her lie, he turned her into a pillar of salt and let the birds peck away at her until all of the salt was gone.

Multiple Choice Study Guide Questions - *Mythology*
Part Five Chapters 17, 18, & 19 continued

5. Why had Agamemnon killed his daughter, Iphigenia?
    A. Zeus appeared to him in a dream and ordered him to do so, to test his loyalty. In reality, it was Hera, getting even with Zeus, who had appeared to him.
    B. She had refused to marry the man he had selected. Agamemnon killed her and her lover.
    C. The Greek army had needed strong winds to sail to Troy. They convinced Agamemnon that if he sacrificed his daughter, the winds would turn in their favor.
    D. He thought that if he sacrificed one of his children to the gods, it would make up for the terrible sins his ancestors had committed.

6. How did Agamemnon die?
    A. He was drowned during a storm at sea.
    B. He was killed by a stray arrow from the bow of Artemis.
    C. He killed himself in grief over the death of his daughter.
    D. His wife killed him.

7. What happened to Clytemnestra and her lover, Aegisthus?
    A. They were banished from Greece and went to live in Ethiopia.
    B. They became the new rulers of the House of Atreus and were very prosperous.
    C. They were killed by her son, Orestes.
    D. They built the best fleet of ships in Greece and became wealthy traders.

8. True or False: Because of Orestes' repentance, the gods established a new law of mercy. They acquitted his house and ended the curse.
    A. True
    B. False

9. What did Cadmus do?
    A. He found his sister, Europa, and returned her to his father's house.
    B. He introduced the principles of mathematics to Greece.
    C. He had six children who all became great leaders in Greece.
    D. He founded the city of Thebes.

10. True or False: Cadmus and harmonia were ultimately rewarded for their good lives.
    A. True
    B. False

Multiple Choice Study Guide Questions - *Mythology*
Part Five Chapters 17, 18, & 19 continued

11. What wrong did Oedipus commit?
    A. He stole the necklace that Hephaestus had given his mother on her wedding day, and gave it to Hera as a present.
    B. He killed the great serpent that had been protecting the city of Thebes.
    C. He killed his father, King Laius, and married his mother, Jocasta.
    D. He gave military secrets to the Trojans.

12. Did he commit this crime knowingly?
    A. Yes, he did.
    B. No, he didn't.

13. What punishment did Oedipus inflict upon himself?
    A. He blinded himself.
    B. He cut out his tongue.
    C. He offered himself as a slave to King Theseus.
    D. He threw himself to a pack of wolves.

14. Why was Antigone killed?
    A. She disobeyed Theseus and gave weapons to the army.
    B. She forced her husband to go to war.
    C. She killed her uncle, Polyneices.
    D. She defied Creon's orders and buried her dead brother, Polyneices.

15. How did Theseus, King of Athens, help Adrastus and the relatives of the chieftains who fought against Thebes?
    A. He took his army into Thebes and forced Creon to allow the dead chieftains a proper burial.
    B. He allowed all of their relatives to become citizens of Athens.
    C. He killed the Thebans who had killed the chieftains.
    D. He conquered Thebes and gave the city to the relatives of the chieftains.

16. For what was Cecrops noted?
    A. He was responsible for Athena becoming the protector of Athens.
    B. He single-handedly built the city of Athens.
    C. He introduced the concept of democracy to the Greek world.
    D. He developed the Greek alphabet and was the first to teach the Greeks to write.

Multiple Choice Study Guide Questions - *Mythology*
Part Five Chapters 17, 18, & 19 continued

17. How did Philomela let Procne know of Tereus' evil deeds?
    A. She sent a message on a scrap of cloth that had been baked into a loaf of bread.
    B. Procne's son had witnessed the deeds and told his mother.
    C. She sang a message to a bird. The bird flew to Procne and sang the message to her.
    D. She wove the story into a tapestry and had the tapestry delivered to Procne.

18. What happened to Procne and Philomela?
    A. The gods granted them places in Olympus because of their suffering.
    B. The gods changed them into birds. Procne became a nightingale. Pilomela became a swallow.
    C. Together they killed Tereus and ruled the country until they died.
    D. They went back to Athens and lived under their father's protection.

19. How did Cephalus test Procris' devotion to him?
    A. He had her servant secretly watch her every move and report to him.
    B. He gave her a pet monkey. The monkey had been trained to imitate her actions upon command from Cephalus.
    C. He disguised himself and tried to make her fall in love with the stranger.
    D. He gave her a truth serum in a glass of wine, then asked her if she had been faithful.

20. True or False: When Cerusa went to the oracle at Delphi, she found out that her son had been found and raised by a man named Xuthus.
    A. True
    B. False

Multiple Choice Study Guide Questions - *Mythology*

Part Six *The Less Important Myths*
Chapter 20 *Midas and Others*   Chapter 21 *Brief Myths*

1. True or False: Midas wished that everything he touched would turn to gold.
    A. True
    B. False

2. For what was Aesculapius honored?
    A. He wrote the first book.
    B. He was the only mortal whom the goddess Artemis loved.
    C. He was a sculptor who made statues of the gods.
    D. He healed the sick.

3. Who were sent to the underworld, where they had to try to carry water in jars filled with holes?
    A. The Pythians
    B. Glaucus and Scylla
    C. The Danaids
    D. Pomona and Vertumnus

4. True or False: Arachne was turned into a spider.
    A. True
    B. False

5. Which human lover of Zeus' was changed into the Great Bear and placed in the sky?
    A. It was Andromeda.
    B. It was Callisto.
    C. It was Coronis.
    D. It was Erysichthon.

6. True or False: The Centaur Chiron was kind and wise. He trained many of the sons of heroes, including Achilles.
    A. True
    B. False

7. From what were the Myrmidons created?
    A. They were created from fish.
    B. They were created from worms.
    C. they were created from grains of sand.
    D. They were created from ants.

Multiple Choice Study Guide Questions - *Mythology*

Part Six Chapters 20 & 21 continued

8. Which great hunter was placed in the sky as a constellation?
    A. It was Orion.
    B. It was Ursinus.
    C. It was Nisus.
    D. It was Linus.

9. True or False: Zeus placed the Pleiades in the sky.
    A. True
    B. False

10. True or False: Salmoneus was sent to Hades to continually roll a rock uphill.
    A. True
    B. False

Multiple Choice Study Guide Questions - *Mythology*

Part 7 *The Mythology of the Norsemen*
Introduction   Chapter 22 *The Stories of Signy and Sigurd*   Chapter 23 *The Norse Gods*

1. What was Asgard like?
    A. It was lovely and warm, and full of flowers.
    B. It was a land of pure white snow. The temperature was comfortable, but the snow never melted.
    C. It was grave and solemn, with a threat of doom always present.
    D. It was mostly unpleasant. The gods were always fighting about which mortals to protect and which to leave alone.

2. True or False: The Norsemen believed that evil would eventually triumph over good.
    A. True
    B. False

3. What was the choice the Norse hero made?
    A. The Norse hero chose between staying and fighting on earth or having a pleasant life in Asgard.
    B. The Norse hero really had no choice; the gods had already chosen him as a hero.
    C. The Norse hero had to choose a god to serve as his protector. If, for some reason, he fell out of favor with that god, none of the others would help him.
    D. The Norse hero chose between yielding to evil or dying for good.

4. What was the name of the hall in Asgard where those who died bravely went?
    A. Niebelungenleid
    B. Volsungasaga
    C. Valhalla
    D. Jotunheim

5. According to Norse mythology, what was the only sustaining support for the human spirit?
    A. It was religion.
    B. It was love.
    C. It was intelligence.
    D. It was heroism.

6. True or False: The central theme of the Norse mythology was that the loser always died.
    A. True
    B. False

Multiple Choice Study Guide Questions - *Mythology*
Part 7 Chapters 22 & 23 continued

7. What was the relationship between Signy and Sigmund?
    A. They were lovers.
    B. They were brother and sister.
    C. They were mother and son.
    D. They were cousins.

8. What did Signy's husband do?
    A. He killed her father and all but one of her brothers.
    B. He killed her lover.
    C. He killed her parents.
    D. He killed her children as they were born.

9. Whose child was Sinfiotli?
    A. He was the child of Signy and Odin.
    B. He was the child of Freya and Sigmund.
    C. He was the child of Signy and Sigmund.
    D. He was the child of Mimir and Volsung.

10. How did Signy get revenge on her husband?
    A. Sigmund and Sinfiotli killed him and Signy's children.
    B. Signy poisoned him.
    C. Signy convinced her children to kill their father.
    D. Sinfiotli killed him, married Signy, and raised the children as his own.

11. Whom did Sigurd rescue?
    A. He rescued Brynhild from a ring of fire.
    B. He rescued his brother Siegfried from Hel.
    C. He rescued Gundrun from the Valkyries.
    D. He rescued Griemhild from Gunnar, her evil husband.

12. How did Sigurd die?
    A. He set himself on fire.
    B. He died of a broken heart.
    C. He was murdered in his sleep.
    D. He sacrificed himself to save one of his enemies.

Multiple Choice Study Guide Questions - *Mythology*
Part Seven   Chapters 22 & 23 continued

13. How did Balder die?
    A. He was killed in a sword fight with Loki.
    B. Odin had Thor strike him with his mighty hammer.
    C. He went to visit the land of the Frost giants and he froze to death.
    D. Hoder threw a twig of poisonous mistletoe which pierced Balder's chest.

14. For what was Odin always searching?
    A. He was always searching for more power.
    B. He was always searching for more wisdom.
    C. He was always searching for more mortals to rule.
    D. He was always searching for justice.

15. Which of the following statements does **not** describe the Valkyries?
    A. They were the daughters of Odin.
    B. They waited on the tables of the gods in Asgard.
    C. They were fierce warriors who hated men.
    D. They went to the battlefield with Odin and decided who would live and die.

16. Which days of the week were named after Norse gods?
    A. Tuesday, Wednesday, Thursday, and Friday were named after Norse gods.
    B. Monday, Wednesday, and Saturday were named after Norse gods.
    C. Sunday, Tuesday, Thursday, and Friday were named after Norse gods.
    D. Only Wednesday was named after a Norse god, Odin.

17. What was the Kingdom of Death called, and who ruled it?
    A. It was ruled by Balder, and was called Balderdash.
    B. It was ruled by Freya, and was called Hel.
    C. It was ruled by Loki, and was called Sleipnir.
    D. It was ruled by Hela, and was called Niflheim.

18. True or False: Odin and his brothers killed their father, the Giant Ymir. They made the earth from his body and the heavens from his skull. They used his blood for the sea.
    A. True
    B. False

Multiple Choice Study Guide Questions - *Mythology*
Part Seven Chapters 22 & 23 continued

19. What did the Norsemen believe would happen after Odin and the other gods were defeated by evil?
    A. They believed that the end of the world would come.
    B. The believed their souls would be carried to the underworld, where they would all live in torment forever.
    C. They believed that another One would come who would triumph over evil.
    D. They believed that evil would eventually consume itself, and a new world would be created.

20. What, according to Hamilton, were the Norsemen's two characteristics?
    A. They were strong but not very bright.
    B. They were heroic and had common sense.
    C. They were religious and adventurous.
    D. They were long-suffering and patient.

21. True or False: Midgard was the area between Asgard and earth where the gods watched over the mortals.
    A. True
    B. False

22 - 25. Matching. Match the following descriptions with the characters being described. Answer choices are given below the descriptions.

22. He was the Thunder-god.

23. She was the Goddess of Love and Beauty.

24. She was Odin's wife.

25. He was the God of War.

   A. Tyr
   B. Freya
   C. Frigga
   D. Thor

ANSWER KEY MULTIPLE CHOICE STUDY GUIDE QUESTIONS *Mythology*

Introduction	Part One Chapters 1&2	Part One Chapters 3&4	Part Two Chapters 5&6	Part Two Chapters 7&8	Part Three Chapters 9-12
1. A. True	1. D.	1. D.	1. B.	1. D.	1. C.
2. C.	2. A.	2. C.	2. B.	2. B. False	2. A. True
3. A. True	3. B. False	3. A.	3. A. True	3. A.	3. C.
4. B.	4. C.	4. A. True	4. A. True	4. C.	4. B. False
5. A.	5. C.	5. B. False	5. C.	5. B. False	5. B.
6. A.	6. D.	6. D.	6. D.	6. A.	6. A.
	7. A.	7. C.	7. C.	7. C.	7. D.
	8. D.	8. B. False	8. A.	8. B.	8. B. False
	9. B. False	9. C.	9. D.	9. B.	9. B.
	10. C.	10. A.	10. B.	10. A.	10. A.
	11. A.	11. D.		11. C.	11. D.
	12. D.	12. D.		12. B.	12. C.
	13. A. True	13. A.		13. B.	13. B. False
	14. D.	14. C.		14. D.	14. D.
	15. B.	15. B.		15. A.	15. C.
	16. C.				
	17. A.				
	18. A. True				
	19. C.				
	20. D.				

Part Four Chapters 13&14	Part Four Chapters 15&16	Part Five Chapters 17,18,19	Part Six Chapters 20&21	Part Seven Chapters 22&23
1. B. False	1. C.	1. D.	1. A.	1. C.
2. A.	2. A.	2. C.	2. D.	2. B. False
3. A. True	3. D.	3. A. True	3. C.	3. D.
4. C.	4. B. False	4. B.	4. D.	4. C.
5. C.	5. C.	5. C.	5. B.	5. D.
6. B.	6. B.	6. D.	6. A. True	6. B. False
7. B. False	7. A.	7. C.	7. D.	7. B.
8. A.	8. A. True	8. A. True	8. A.	8. A.
9. B. False	9. B.	9. D.	9. A.	9. C.
10. A.	10. D.	10. B. False	10. B.	10. A.
	11. C.	11. C.		11. A.
	12. C.	12. B.		12. C.
	13. A. True	13. A.		13. D.
	14. D.	14. D.		14. B.
	15. B.	15. A.		15. C.
		16. A.		16. A.

Answer Key Multiple Choice Study Guide Questions Continued

Part Five
Chapters 17,18,19
17. D.
18. B.
19. C.
20. B. False

Part Seven
Chapters 22&23
17. D.
18. A. True
19. C.
20. B.
21. B. False
22. D.
23. B.
24. C.
25. A.

PRE-READING VOCABULARY WORKSHEETS

Pre-reading Vocabulary Worksheets - *Mythology*

SPECIAL MYTHOLOGICAL TERMS

Introduction Part I: Using Prior Knowledge and Context Clues
Below are the sentences in which the vocabulary words appear in the text. Read the sentence. Use any clues you can find in the sentence combined with your prior knowledge, and write what you think the underlined words mean on the lines provide.

1. Greek and Roman mythology is quite generally supposed to show us the way the human race thought and felt untold years ago.
_____

2 & 3. Anyone in the woods might see through the trees a fleeing nymph, or bending over a clear pool to drink, behold in the depths a naiad's face.
_____

_____

4. In Egypt, a towering colossus, immobile, beyond the power of the imagination to endow with movement.
_____

5. Nevertheless he was not omnipotent or omniscient either. He could be opposed and deceived.
_____

6. ...a humanized world, men freed from the paralyzing fear of an omnipotent Unknown.
_____

7. The fauns were Roman satyrs.
_____

8 & 9. Dwelling in Olympus, they are happy all their days, feasting upon nectar and ambrosia.
_____

_____

10. The dryad who would have perished with it told him to ask anything he desired and she would give it to him.
_____

Pre-reading Vocabulary Worksheets - *Mythology*

Special Mythological Terms continued

Part II: Determining the Meaning   Match the vocabulary words to their dictionary definitions.

____ 1. mythology   A. all-powerful

____ 2. nymph   B. stories of the origin of a people, their gods, and heroes

____ 3. naiad   C. the food of the gods, thought to give immortality

____ 4. colossus   D. having a human body with ears, legs, and horns of a goat

____ 5. omniscient   E. knowing everything

____ 6. omnipotent   F. a female spirit that represents nature

____ 7. satyrs   G. the drink of the gods; the undiluted juice of a fruit

____ 8. nectar   H. a spirit that lives in brooks and springs

____ 9. ambrosia   I. a huge statue

____10. dryad   J. a wood nymph

Pre-reading Vocabulary Worksheets - *Mythology*

Part One *The Gods, The Creation, and the Earliest Heroes*
Chapter 1 *The Gods*   Chapter 2 *The Two Great Gods of Earth*

Introduction Part I: Using Prior Knowledge and Context Clues

Below are the sentences in which the vocabulary words appear in the text. Read the sentence. Use any clues you can find in the sentence combined with your prior knowledge, and write what you think the underlined words mean on the lines provided.

1. He was unpitying, inexorable, but just; a terrible, not an evil god.
___

2. Even more than of these good and lovely endowments, he is the God of Light.
___

3. They clad her in raiment immortal.
___

4. Homer calls him murderous, bloodstained, the incarnate curse of mortals.
___

5. He never was to them the mean whining deity of the Iliad, but magnificent in shining armor, redoubtable, invincible.
___

6. Quirinus was the name of the deified Romulus, the founder of Rome.
___

7. ...Zeus a dangerous lover for mortal maidens and completely incalculable in his use of the terrible thunderbolt.
___

8. When they were not positively harmful they were capricious and undependable.
___

9. In her desolate wanderings she came to Eleusis and sat by the wayside near a well.
___

Pre-reading Vocabulary Worksheets - *Mythology*
Part One Chapters 1 & 2 continued

10. He was accompanied, as was his custom, by a train of women dancing and singing <u>exultant</u> songs.
_____

Part II: Determining the Meaning   Match the vocabulary words to their dictionary definitions.

____ 1. inexorable   A. given human form

____ 2. endowments   B. unpredictable; impossible to foresee

____ 3. raiment   C. not able to be persuaded

____ 4. incarnate   D. clothing

____ 5. redoubtable   E. barren, lifeless

____ 6. deified   F. joyful, triumphant

____ 7. incalculable   G. a fund donated to a group or individual

____ 8. capricious   H. impulsive; given to whim

____ 9. desolate   I. arousing fear or awe

____10. exultant   J. worshipped as a god

Pre-reading Vocabulary Worksheets - *Mythology*
Part One *The Gods, The Creation, and the Earliest Heroes*
Chapter 3 *How the World and Mankind Were Created*   Chapter 4 *The Earliest Heroes*

Introduction Part I: Using Prior Knowledge and Context Clues
Below are the sentences in which the vocabulary words appear in the text. Read the sentence. Use any clues you can find in the sentence combined with your prior knowledge, and write what you think the underlined words mean on the lines provided.

1. Erebus is the <u>unfathomable</u> depth where death dwells.
_____

2. Groans shall your speech be, <u>lamentation</u> your only words.
_____

3. It looked like a <u>heifer,</u> but talked like a girl who seemed mad with misery.
_____

4. You-he who <u>succored</u> the whole race of men?
_____

5. Swells on a ship, and ever gently thus they <u>wafted</u> her.
_____

6. He bade each man choose out three rams and bind them with strong, <u>pliant</u> strips of bark.
_____

7. Her voice would ring in his ears calling him a <u>laggard</u> in love.
_____

8. The contrast of this laughing, luxuriant beauty with the clear-cut, <u>austere</u> grandeur all around arrests the attention sharply.

Part II: Determining the Meaning   Match the vocabulary words to their dictionary definitions.

____ 1. unfathomable   A. assisted, helped
____ 2. lamentation   B. floated gently and smoothly
____ 3. heifer   C. severe, having no decoration
____ 4. succored   D. not able to be understood
____ 5. wafted   E. a song or poem that expresses grief or mourning
____ 6. pliant   F. easily bent
____ 7. laggard   G. straggler
____ 8. austere   H. a young cow, especially one that has not given birth

Pre-reading Vocabulary Worksheets - *Mythology*

Part Two *Stories of Love and Adventure*
Chapter 5 *Cupid and Psyche*   Chapter 6 *Eight Brief Tales of Lovers*

Introduction Part I: Using Prior Knowledge and Context Clues
Below are the sentences in which the vocabulary words appear in the text. Read the sentence. Use any clues you can find in the sentence combined with your prior knowledge, and write what you think the underlined words mean on the lines provided.

1. She seemed a very goddess consorting with mere mortals.
_____

2. ...to do her homage as though she were in truth one of the immortals.
_____

3. "But really," she said, "you are so plain and ill-favored a girl that you will never be able to get you a lover except by the most diligent and painful service."
_____

4. No; he was a horrible serpent and she loathed him.
_____

5. She offered ardent prayers to them perpetually, but not one of them would do anything.
_____

6. The conclusion was inevitable.
_____

7. She ventured to go back to the tree of the tryst, the mulberry with the shining white fruit.
_____

8. She determined to help a young man who could be enamored and yet original.
_____

9. The alliance had become eminently suitable.
_____

10. Such was the wondrous power of this disdainful young man.
_____

Pre-reading Vocabulary Worksheets - *Mythology*
Part Two Chapters 5&6 continued

Part II: Determining the Meaning   Match the vocabulary words to their dictionary definitions.

____ 1. consorting   A. detested

____ 2. homage   B. lasting for an unlimited time

____ 3. diligent   C. impossible to avoid

____ 4. loathed   D. outstanding, distinguished, of high quality

____ 5. perpetually   E. a meeting arranged by lovers

____ 6. inevitable   F. marked by careful, persistent effort

____ 7. tryst   G. honor or respect that is shown publicly

____ 8. enamored   H. associating with

____ 9. eminently   I. inspired with love

____ 10. disdainful   J. showing contempt

Pre-reading Vocabulary Worksheets - *Mythology*

Part Two *Stories of Love and Adventure*
Chapter 7 *The Quest of the Golden Fleece*   Chapter 8 *Four Great Adventures*

Introduction Part I: Using Prior Knowledge and Context Clues
Below are the sentences in which the vocabulary words appear in the text. Read the sentence. Use any clues you can find in the sentence combined with your prior knowledge, and write what you think the underlined words mean on the lines provided.

1. However, they were all heroes of renown, and they were quite equal to their adventures.
_____

2.&3. The usurper Pelias had been told by an oracle that he would die at the hands of a kinsman.
_____
_____

4. And now both were fixing their eyes on the ground abashed.
_____

5. If I can make your baseness manifest.
_____

6. She was a most singular portent, a lion in front, a serpent behind, a goat in between.
_____

7. He is a very pedestrian writer.
_____

8. The torrent of Medea's wrongs burst forth.
_____

Part II: Determining the Meaning   Match the vocabulary words to their dictionary definitions.

____ 1. renown   A. a turbulent or overwhelming flow
____ 2. usurper   B. clear, understandable
____ 3. oracle   C. fame
____ 4. abashed   D. ordinary, not imaginative
____ 5. manifest   E. one who takes another's place or authority by force
____ 6. portent   F. sign, forewarning, omen
____ 7. pedestrian   G. embarrassed
____ 8. torrent   H. the transmitter of prophecies at a shrine

Pre-reading Vocabulary Worksheets - *Mythology*
Part Three *The Great Heroes Before the Trojan War*
Chapter 9 *Perseus*   Chapter 10 *Theseus*   Chapter 11 *Hercules*   Chapter 12 *Atalanta*

Introduction Part I: Using Prior Knowledge and Context Clues
Below are the sentences in which the vocabulary words appear in the text. Read the sentence. Use any clues you can find in the sentence combined with your prior knowledge, and write what you think the underlined words mean on the lines provided.

1. The scudding waves so near your soft curls.
_____

2. ...to sail on it would be a contemptible flight from danger.
_____

3. He spent a large part of his life expiating one unfortunate deed after another.
_____

4. Sometimes he punished himself when others were inclined to exonerate him.
_____

5. It would have been ludicrous to put him in command of a kingdom.
_____

6. He was helped by Athena to drive them out of their coverts, and as they flew up he shot them.
_____

7. One of the poems ascribed to Hesiod describes the race and the golden apples.
_____

8. ...who loved adventure as much as the most dauntless hero.
_____

Part II: Determining the Meaning   Match the vocabulary words to their dictionary definitions.

____ 1. scudding   A. absurd, incongruous
____ 2. contemptible   B. skimming along swiftly and easily
____ 3. expiating   C. attributed to
____ 4. exonerate   D. fearless, not intimidated
____ 5. ludicrous   E. to free from blame
____ 6. coverts   F. despicable
____ 7. ascribed   G. making amends, atoning
____ 8. dauntless   H. thick underbrush offering shelter for game

Pre-reading Vocabulary Worksheets - *Mythology*

Part Four *The Heroes of the Trojan War*
Chapter 13 *The Trojan War*   Chapter 14 *The Fall of Troy*

Introduction Part I: Using Prior Knowledge and Context Clues
Below are the sentences in which the vocabulary words appear in the text. Read the sentence. Use any clues you can find in the sentence combined with your prior knowledge, and write what you think the underlined words mean on the lines provided.

1. Her reputed father, King Tyndareus, her mother's husband, was afraid to select one.

2. Her thoughts were busy as to how she might help the Greeks and circumvent Zeus.

3. But Diomedes raged on, working havoc in the Trojan ranks.

4. A brother of Hector's, wise in discerning the will of the gods, urged Hector to go with all speed to the city.

5. "Try to find some way of appeasing him," he said, "instead of going home disgraced."

6. Patroclus, Achilles' beloved friend, saw the rout with horror.

7. She was to tell him that violent as Achilles was, he was not really evil, but one who could treat properly a suppliant.

8. His name was Sinon, and he was a most plausible speaker.

9. He was a pious youth with the most admirable filial sentiments.

10. The wooden horse had been made, as he said, as a votive offering to Athena.

Pre-reading Vocabulary Worksheets - *Mythology*
Part Four Chapters 13 & 14 continued

Part II: Determining the Meaning   Match the vocabulary words to their dictionary definitions.

____ 1. reputed   A. relating to a son or daughter

____ 2. circumvent   B. a disorderly retreat following a defeat

____ 3. havoc   C. distinguishing, perceiving as being different

____ 4. discerning   D. to go around or bypass

____ 5. appeasing   E. an offering given to fulfill a vow

____ 6. rout   F. asking humbly

____ 7. suppliant   G. devastation, chaos

____ 8. plausible   H. soothing, pacifying

____ 9. filial   I. supposed, considered

____10. votive   J. having some truth, but still open to doubt

Pre-reading Vocabulary Worksheets - *Mythology*

Part Four *The Heroes of the Trojan War*
Chapter 15 *The Adventures of Odysseus*   Chapter 16 *The Adventures of Aeneas*

Introduction Part I: Using Prior Knowledge and Context Clues
Below are the sentences in which the vocabulary words appear in the text. Read the sentence. Use any clues you can find in the sentence combined with your prior knowledge, and write what you think the underlined words mean on the lines provided.

1. She enticed into her house the party Odysseus dispatched to spy out the land.

2. She treated them with kindness, feasting them sumptuously in her house.

3. So rang their song in lovely cadences.

4. He succeeded in reaching the Phaeacian land, a helpless destitute man.

5. An angry clamor broke out at the words.

6. Virgil is responsible for the change from the human Aeneas of the first books to the unhuman prodigy of the last.

7. ...and reaching Italy far to the north of the whirlpool of implacable Charybdis.

8. ...his face squalid in the extreme with a thick growth of hair.

9. She was known to be not susceptible. All the kings of the country had tried to persuade her to marry them with no success.

10. The king went forth with two great dogs following him, his sole retinue and bodyguard.

Pre-reading Vocabulary Worksheets - *Mythology*
Part Four Chapters 15 & 16 continued

Part II: Determining the Meaning Match the vocabulary words to their dictionary definitions.

____ 1. enticed   A. messengers, government representatives

____ 2. sumptuously   B. balanced, rhythmic beats

____ 3. cadences   C. a person who has exceptional talents or powers

____ 4. destitute   D. dirty from poverty or lack of care

____ 5. clamor   E. lavishly, suggesting great expense

____ 6. prodigy   F. impoverished, lacking the means of subsistence

____ 7. implacable   G. lured, tempted

____ 8. squalid   H. loud expression of discontent

____ 9. susceptible   I. not able to be appeased

____ 10. retinue   J. easily affected or influenced

Pre-reading Vocabulary Worksheets - *Mythology*

Part Five *The Great Families of Mythology*
Chapter 17 *The House of Atreus*   Chapter 18 *The Royal House of Thebes*
Chapter 19 *The House of Athens*

Introduction part I: Using Prior Knowledge and Context Clues
Below are the sentences in which the vocabulary words appear in the text. Read the sentence. Use any clues you can find in the sentence combined with your prior knowledge, and write what you think the underlined words mean on the lines provided.

1. In return for their favor he acted so atrociously that no poet ever tried to explain his conduct.
_____

2. One of the goddesses inadvertently had eaten some of the loathsome dish.
_____

3. It was a sordid tale.
_____

4. He learned that no crime was beyond atonement, that even he could be made clean.
_____

5. With the words of acquittal, the spirit of evil which had haunted his house was banished.
_____

6. Whatever the priestess at Delphi said would happen infallibly came to pass.
_____

7. It seemed, nevertheless, that nothing could be done except to acquiesce.
_____

8. In return for this good gift, Cecrops, who had been made arbiter, decided that Athena was hers.
_____

9. In one story of this contest between the two deities, woman's suffrage plays a part.
_____

10. But the men, along with Poseidon, were greatly chagrined at this female triumph.
_____

Pre-reading Vocabulary Worksheets - *Mythology*
Part Five Chapters 17, 18, & 19 continued

Part II: Determining the Meaning Match the vocabulary words to their dictionary definitions.

____ 1. atrociously   A. morally degraded

____ 2. inadvertently   B. horribly, cruelly

____ 3. sordid   C. making amends for an injury or wrong

____ 4. atonement   D. a judge

____ 5. acquittal   E. accidentally

____ 6. infallibly   F. not capable of an error

____ 7. acquiesce   G. the right to vote

____ 8. arbiter   H. a freeing or clearing from a charge or accusation

____ 9. suffrage   I. embarrassed due to failure or disappointment

____ 10. chagrined   J. to consent without protest

Pre-reading Vocabulary Worksheets - *Mythology*

Part Six *The Less Important Myths*
Chapter 20 *Midas and Others*   Chapter 21 *Brief Myths Arranged Alphabetically*

Introduction Part I: Using Prior Knowledge and Context Clues
Below are the sentences in which the vocabulary words appear in the text. Read the sentence. Use any clues you can find in the sentence combined with your prior knowledge, and write what you think the underlined words mean on the lines provided.

1. The fat old drunkard was found asleep in a bower of roses.
_____

2. She fled from him until she stood on a lofty promontory where she could safely watch him.
_____

3. Her story is the only one in which the good goddess Ceres appears cruel and vindictive.
_____

4. Erysichthon had the wicked audacity to cut down the tallest oak in a grove sacred to Ceres.
_____

5.&6. He learned in this way the art of divination as no one ever had, and he became a famous soothsayer.
_____
_____

7. Hera sent a fearful pestilence which destroyed the people by thousands.
_____

8. He found a pang of grief as he watched the maiden placed on the funeral pyre and the wild flames roar up.
_____

9. This man was another illustration of how fatal it was for mortals to try to emulate the gods.
_____

Pre-reading Vocabulary Worksheets - *Mythology*
Part Six Chapters 20 & 21 continued

Part II: Determining the Meaning   Match the vocabulary words to their dictionary definitions.

____ 1. bower   A. a shaded, leafy recess or arbor

____ 2. promontory   B. to compete with successfully

____ 3. vindictive   C. daring, boldness

____ 4. audacity   D. a pile of things that can be used for burning corpses

____ 5. divination   E. unforgiving, seeking revenge

____ 6. soothsayer   F. a fatal epidemic disease

____ 7. pestilence   G. the art of foretelling events by use of the supernatural

____ 8. pyre   H. a high ridge of land that juts out into the water

____ 9. emulate   I. a prophet

Pre-reading Vocabulary Worksheets - *Mythology*

Part Seven *The Mythology of the Norsemen*
Introduction   Chapter 22 *The Stories of Signy and of Sigurd*   Chapter 23 *The Norse Gods*

Introduction Part I: Using Prior Knowledge and Context Clues
Below are the sentences in which the vocabulary words appear in the text. Read the sentence. Use any clues you can find in the sentence combined with your prior knowledge, and write what you think the underlined words mean on the lines provided.

1. This is the conception of life which underlies the Norse religion, as somber a conception as the mind of man has ever given birth to.
   _____

2. The only sustaining support possible for the human spirit, the one pure unsullied good men can hope to attain is heroism.
   _____

3. The story of Siegfried is so familiar that that of his Norse prototype, Sigurd, can be briefly told.
   _____

4. ... and all the sorrow of the world was turned to futility, for she refused to weep.
   _____

5. This vision of a happiness infinitely remote seems a thin sustenance against despair.
   _____

6. A paltry man and poor of mind is he who mocks at all things.
   _____

Part II: Determining the Meaning   Match the vocabulary words to their dictionary definitions.

____ 1. somber   A. trivial, lacking in importance
____ 2. unsullied   B. frivolous, having no useful result
____ 3. prototype   C. not stained or tainted
____ 4. futility   D. gloomy, depressing
____ 5. sustenance   E. an original that serves as a model
____ 6. paltry   F. the supporting of life or health

Pre-reading Vocabulary Worksheets - *Mythology*

ANSWER KEY - VOCABULARY - *Mythology*

Special Terms	Chapters 1&2	Chapters 3&4	Chapters 5&6
1. B.	1. C.	1. D.	1. H.
2. F.	2. G.	2. E.	2. G.
3. H.	3. D.	3. H.	3. F.
4. I.	4. A.	4. A.	4. A.
5. E.	5. I.	5. B.	5. B.
6. A.	6. J.	6. F.	6. C.
7. D.	7. B.	7. G.	7. E.
8. G.	8. H.	8. C.	8. I.
9. C.	9. E.		9. D.
10. J.	10. F.		10. J.

Chapters 7&8	Chapters 9,10,11,12	Chapters 13&14	Chapters 15&16
1. C.	1. B.	1. I.	1. G.
2. E.	2. F.	2. D.	2. E.
3. H.	3. G.	3. G.	3. B.
4. G.	4. E.	4. C.	4. F.
5. B.	5. A.	5. H.	5. H.
6. F.	6. H.	6. B.	6. C.
7. D.	7. C.	7. F.	7. I.
8. A.	8. D.	8. J.	8. D.
		9. A.	9. J.
		10. E.	10. A.

Chapters 17,18,&19	Chapters 20&21	Mythology of the Norsemen
1. B.	1. A.	1. D.
2. E.	2. H.	2. C.
3. A.	3. E.	3. E.
4. C.	4. C.	4. B.
5. H.	5. G.	5. F.
6. F.	6. I.	6. A.
7. J.	7. F.	
8. D.	8. D.	
9. G.	9. B.	
10. I.		

DAILY LESSONS

LESSON ONE - *Mythology*

Objectives
> 1. To introduce the *Mythology* unit
> 2. To give students some background information about Hamilton and her works
> 3. To watch a filmstrip/video pertaining to one or more of the myths presented in *Mythology*
> 4. To explain and assign Writing Assignment 1

Activity #1

Do a group KWL Sheet with the students (form included.) Many students will know something about mythology and will have information to share. Put this information in the K column (what I know.) Ask students what they want to find out, and put it in the W column (what I want to find out.) Keep the sheet and refer to it after reading the book, and complete the L column (what I learned.) Students may also enjoy talking about other myths they have heard.

Activity #2

Show a film (strip)/video about one or more of the stories from the *Mythology* book. You may want students to use the video note-taking form while they are watching it. The form is purposely generic, because there are many different films available.

Activity #3

Distribute the materials students will use in this unit. Explain in detail how students are to use these materials.

Study Guides   Students should preview the study guide questions before each reading assignment to get a feeling for what events and ideas are important in that section. After reading the section, students will (as a class or individually) answer the questions to review the important events and ideas from that section of the book. Students should keep the study guides as study materials for the unit test.

Reading Assignment Sheet You need to fill in the reading assignment sheet to let students know when their reading has to be completed. You can either write the assignment sheet on a side blackboard or bulletin board and leave it there for students to see each day, or you can "ditto" copies for each student to have. In either case, you should advise students to become very familiar with the reading assignments so they know what is expected of them.

Extra Activities Center The resource sections of this unit contain suggestions for a library of related books and articles in your classroom as well as crossword and word search puzzles. Make an extra activities center in your room where you will keep these materials for students to use. (Bring the books and articles in from the library and keep several copies of the puzzles on hand.) Explain to students that these materials are available for students to use when they finish reading assignments or other class work early.

<u>Books</u>   Each school has its own rules and regulations regarding student use of school books. Advise students of the procedures that are normal for your school.

<u>Activity #4</u>
Distribute Writing Assignment #1. Go over the directions and the topics with the students. You may want to use only the Critical/Personal Response and Personal Response questions for this assignment. The Interpretive and Critical questions can be used later on as class discussion questions.

KWL - *Mythology*

Directions: Before reading, think about what you already know about Edith Hamilton and/or *Mythology*. Write the information in the K column. Think about what you would like to find out from reading the book. Write your questions in the W column. After you have read the book, use the L column to write the answers to your questions from the W column, and anything else you remember from the book.

K What I Know	W What I Want To Find Out	L What I Learned

FILMSTRIP/VIDEO NOTE-TAKING FORM - *Mythology*

Directions: Use this form to help yourself remember information from the film. Read the categories before watching the film. Then, while you are watching, record important information in the appropriate column. You may want to check with classmates after you are finished, and share your information.

About Edith Hamilton	About *Mythology*	Other Information

WRITING ASSIGNMENT #1- *Mythology*

Student's Name_____Class_____

PROMPT

    Your assignment is to answer the question number _____from the list entitled EXTRA WRITING ASSIGNMENTS/DISCUSSION QUESTIONS.

PRE-WRITING

    You are being given this assignment now so that as you read *Mythology* you can pay particular attention to the parts which may help you answer your questions.

    As you read the book, you will probably think, "Oh, this part could have something to do with my question." When you come across examples or ideas like that, jot them down on a piece of paper--whether it is a page reference in your book or an idea which pops into your head--write it down. This will make the actual writing of the paper easier.

DRAFTING

    You should begin with an introductory paragraph giving your reader the topic of your paper. Change the question you are answering into a statement, and use this as an introduction.

    The body of your composition should contain information related to your question. You may want to summarize a section of the book, or briefly retell an event. You may also use direct quotes from the novel. If you do this, use quotation marks around each quote, and make sure to cite each one at the end of the quote. (Example: Hamilton, page 112.)

    Write a paragraph in which you restate your topic and summarize your conclusions.

PROMPT

    When you finish the rough draft of your paper, ask a student who sits near you to read it. After reading your rough draft, he/she should tell you what he/she liked best about your work, which parts were difficult to understand, and ways in which your work could be improved. Reread your paper considering your critic's comments, and make the corrections you think are necessary.

PROOFREADING

    Do a final proofreading of your paper double-checking your grammar, spelling, organization, and the clarity of your ideas.

    After your paper is written, you will be asked to give a summary of your answer in order to lead a class discussion of the topic your question examines.

EXTRA WRITING ASSIGNMENTS AND/OR DISCUSSION QUESTIONS
Mythology

<u>Interpretive</u>
1. What do the myths show us about the human race of long ago?

2. Could the myths be set in a different time and place and still have the same effect?

3. What were the original writers of the myths (not Hamilton) trying to show by having Zeus fall in love with so many mortal women?

4. How did the persona of Zeus change over the course of the myths?

5. What does the behavior of Hera tell you about her?

6. What did the new belief in Dionysus show about the Greeks of the time? (Chapter 2)

7. Why were Aphrodite, Hera, and Pallas Athena willing to accept the judgment of a mortal man, Paris? (Chapter 13)

8. What does Achilles' treatment of Hector's body tell you about Achilles? (Chapter 13)

<u>Critical</u>
9. Describe Hamilton's writing style. How does it influence your understanding of the various myths?

10. Compare and contrast the gods (in general) of the Greek/Roman myths with those of the Norse myths.

11. Compare and contrast one specific Greek/Roman god or goddess with the Norse counterpart.

12. Compare and contrast the Greek/Roman and the Norse creation myths.

13. Analyze the character of one of the following deities: Zeus, Hera, Artemis, Athena, Cupid, Prometheus.

14. Analyze the character of one of the following heroes: Paris, Hercules, Theseus, Jason, Odysseus, Sigurd.

EXTRA WRITING ASSIGNMENTS AND/OR DISCUSSION QUESTIONS - *Mythology*
continued

Critical continued

15. Discuss the role of women in the myths.

16. If you have read another interpretation of the myths, compare and contrast it with Hamilton's.

17. What did the Greek and Trojan responses to the kidnapping of Helen tell you about the two societies?

18. Hamilton says that the two main characteristics of the Norsemen were heroism and common sense. Do you agree or disagree? Cite examples from the reading to support your answer.

19. Why do you think the Greek/Roman and the Norse views of the afterlife were so different?

20. Why do you think people needed the myths?

Critical/Personal Response

21. Which of the deities seems the most important to you? Support your answer with examples from the text.

22. Hamilton says that Dionysus was the only god whose parents were not both divine. Why do you think he was accepted as a god?

23. The expression "beware of Greeks bearing gifts" is sometimes used today. To which myth does it relate? Is it an appropriate reference?

24. Do you agree with the judgment of Paris made in Chapter 13? If you were the judge, what would you do?

Personal Response

25. If you could be any character in the book for a short time, which one would you choose? Why?

26. Do you think the myths have influenced modern day belief systems? If so, how? If not, why not?

EXTRA WRITING ASSIGNMENTS AND/OR DISCUSSION QUESTIONS - *Mythology*
continued

<u>Personal Response continued</u>

27. If you could re-name the days of the week after different deities, which would you choose?

28. Which was your favorite deity or hero? Why?

29. If you were writing the myths, how would you portray the deities?

30. Why do you think the early writers created so many gods and goddesses?

LESSON TWO - *Mythology*

Objectives
1. To complete the pre-reading work for the Introduction and Part One, Chapters 1 & 2
2. To begin reading *Mythology*
3. To give students the opportunity to practice their oral reading skills
4. To give the teacher an opportunity to evaluate students' reading abilities
5. To review the main idea and details in Part One, Chapters 1 & 2

Activity #1

Work with students to complete the pre-reading work for the Introduction and Part One, Chapters 1 & 2 of *Mythology*. They should review the study questions and do the required vocabulary work. You may want to make this a whole-class activity if they have not used this format previously.

Activity #2

Read the introduction aloud to the class to model correct oral reading techniques. Have students begin reading *Mythology*, Part One, Chapter 1 orally. You probably know the best way to get readers within your class; pick students at random, ask for volunteers, or use whatever method works best for your group. If you have not yet completed an oral reading evaluation for your students this marking period, this would be a good opportunity to do so. A form is included with this unit for your convenience. You may want to spread this out over two days to give each student ample reading time.

Activity #3

Give students time to answer the study guide questions. Write the answers on the board or overhead transparency so students can have the correct answers for study purposes. Note: It is a good practice in public speaking and leadership skills for individual students to take charge of leading the discussions of the study questions. Perhaps a different student could go to the front of the class and lead the discussion each day that the study questions are discussed during this unit. Of course, the teacher should guide the discussion when appropriate and be sure to fill in any gaps the students leave.

ORAL READING EVALUATION - *Mythology*

Name_____Class_____Date_____

SKILL	EXCELLENT	GOOD	AVERAGE	FAIR	POOR
Fluency	5	4	3	2	1
Clarity	5	4	3	2	1
Audibility	5	4	3	2	1
Pronunciation	5	4	3	2	1
_____	5	4	3	2	1
_____	5	4	3	2	1

Total_____Grade_____

Comments:

LESSON THREE - *Mythology*

Objectives
1. To complete the pre-reading work for Part One, Chapters 3 & 4
2. To give students the opportunity to practice their oral reading skills
3. To give the teacher an opportunity to evaluate students' reading abilities
4. To review the main ideas and events from Part One, Chapters 3 & 4
5. To practice re-reading to locate specific information

Activity #1

Have students complete the pre-reading work for Part One, Chapters 3 & 4.

Activity #2

If you did not complete the oral reading evaluations from Lesson One, finish them today. If the oral reading evaluations have been completed, have the students read silently.

Activity #3

Give students a few minutes to formulate answers for the study guide questions for Part One, Chapters 3 & 4. Use the same procedure as in Lesson One to review the answers with the class.

Activity #4

If necessary, demonstrate how to re-read to locate information in the text. Suggest to the students that they indicate the page number where they found each answer on their study question sheet or in their notebook. If students own the books, you may want to show them how to highlight specific information and make margin notes.

LESSON FOUR - *Mythology*

Objectives
1. To assign and discuss the Nonfiction Assignment Sheet
2. To give the students some time to work on their nonfiction assignments
3. To give students the opportunity to browse in the library and read about some topics that interest them.

**Depending on your particular situation, you may want to conduct the entire class in the library, or discuss the Nonfiction Assignment Sheet in the classroom and then go to the library.

Activity #1

Nonfiction Assignment Sheet Explain to students that they each are to read at least one nonfiction piece from the in-class library at some time during the unit. Students will fill out a nonfiction assignment sheet after completing the reading to help you (the teacher) evaluate their reading experiences and to help the students think about and evaluate their own reading experiences.

Activity #2

Take your students to the library. Tell them that the purpose for their being at the library is to find appropriate materials to complete the nonfiction reading assignment they have just received. Give students ample time to find materials and begin reading.
Suggested topics:
1. Articles of criticism about Mythology
2. A biography of Edith Hamilton
3. The history of Ancient Greece
4. The history of Ancient Rome
5. The history of the ancient Norsemen
6. An atlas of the ancient world
7. Articles or books about ancient religions
8. Greek philosophy (for your advanced students)

NONFICTION ASSIGNMENT SHEET - *Mythology*
(To be completed after reading the required nonfiction article)

Name_____Date_____Class_____

Title of Nonfiction Read_____

Written By _____Publication Date_____

1. Factual Summary: Write a short summary of the piece you read.

II. Vocabulary:
    1. With which vocabulary words in the piece did you encounter some degree of difficulty?

    2. How did you resolve your lack of understanding with these words?

III. Interpretation: What was the main point the author wanted you to get from reading his/her work?

IV. Criticism:
    1. With which points of the piece did you agree or find easy to accept? Why?

    2. With which points of the piece did you disagree or find difficult to believe? Why?

V. Personal Response: What do you think about this piece? OR How does this piece influence your ideas?

LESSON FIVE - *Mythology*

Objectives
1. To complete the pre-reading work for Part Two, Chapters 5 & 6
2. To silently read Part Two, Chapters 5 & 6
3. To review the main events from Part Two, Chapters 5 & 6
4. To assign pre-reading work and reading for Part Three, Chapters 9-12

Activity #1
Have students review the study questions, do the required vocabulary work, and then read the assigned chapters.

Activity #2
Have students continue working in pairs. Assign each pair of students a few study guide questions to answer. Have each pair present their answers aloud for the class.

Activity #3
Assign the pre-reading work, reading, and study questions for Part Three, Chapters 9-12. Allow two class days for completion of the assignment.

Activity #4
Tell students they will be having a quiz on the Introduction and Chapters 1-12. Give the date for the quiz (see Lesson Eight.)

LESSON SIX - *Mythology*

Objectives
1. To complete the pre-reading work for Part Two, Chapters 7 & 8
2. To give students the opportunity to practice their oral reading skills
3. To give students the opportunity to practice their listening skills
4. To review the main ideas and events of Part Two, Chapters 7 & 8

Activity #1
Have students review the study questions and do the required vocabulary work.

Activity #2
Tell students they will be reading aloud in pairs. One partner will listen and follow along in their book while the other reads aloud. They should switch off frequently. Assign partners, or allow students to choose their partners.

Activity #3
Have students answer the study questions individually, and then check their answers with a classmate.

LESSON SEVEN - *Mythology*

Objectives
    1. To review the main ideas and events of Part Three, Chapters 9-12
    2. To use cooperative learning strategies to study for a quiz

Activity #1
    Review the answers to the study questions with the whole class. Encourage students to correct their answers and take notes in preparation for the quiz.

Activity #2
    Tell students they will be having a quiz during the next class period. Have the students work with partners to review the study guide questions from the Introduction through Chapter 12 in preparation for the quiz.

LESSON EIGHT - *Mythology*

Objectives
    1. To demonstrate understanding of the material by successfully completing a quiz
    2. To do the pre-reading work for Part Four, Chapters 13 & 14
    3. To read silently Part Four, Chapters 13 & 14

Activity #1
    Distribute copies of the quiz. You may want to use some of the Multiple Choice questions for this purpose.

Activity #2
    Allow students to begin the work for Chapters 13 & 14 as soon as they are finished with the quiz. Have them finish the assignment at home if they do not complete it in class.

LESSON NINE - *Mythology*

Objectives
1. To review the main ideas and events from Part Four, Chapters 13 & 14
2. To do the pre-reading work for Part Four, Chapters 15 & 16
3. To silently read Part Four, Chapters 15 & 16

Activity #1
Review the answers to the study questions for Chapters 13 & 14. Encourage students to re-read the text if necessary to find the correct answers.

Activity #2
Allow students to work with partners to complete the pre-reading work for part Four, Chapters 15 & 16. Give students the remainder of the period to complete the pre-reading work and begin reading the chapters. Allow student who wish to read aloud to each other to do so quietly.

If students do not finish reading Chapters 15 & 16 in class, they should do so before the next class meeting.

LESSON TEN - *Mythology*

Objectives
1. To review the main ideas and events from Part Four, Chapters 15 & 16
2. To discuss *Mythology* on interpretive and critical levels.

Activity #1
Allow students to work with a small group to check the answers to the study questions for Chapters 15 & 16. Remind them to refer to the text if necessary. Provide assistance with any difficult questions.

Activity #2
Choose the questions from the Interpretive and Critical Levels of the Extra Discussion Questions/Writing Assignments which seem most appropriate for your students. A class discussion of these questions is most effective if students have been given the opportunity to formulate answers to the questions prior to the discussion. To this end, you may either have all the students formulate answers to all the questions, divide your class into groups and assign one or more questions to each group, or you could assign one question to each student in your class. The option you choose will make a difference in the amount of class time needed for this activity.

Activity #3
After students have had ample time to formulate answers to the questions, begin your class discussion of the questions and the ideas presented by the questions. Be sure students take notes during the discussion so they have information to study for the unit test.

LESSON ELEVEN - *Mythology*

Objective
> To give students the opportunity to practice their writing skills

Activity #1
> Distribute Writing Assignment #2 and discuss the directions in detail. Introduce the Writing Evaluation Form and discuss its purpose. You may want to distribute copies of it, or have the students copy the information into their notebooks. Encourage them to refer to the Evaluation Form as they are editing and revising their papers.

Activity #2
> Allow students to use the remainder of the class period to work on the assignment. Tell students their first drafts will be due in two class periods (Lesson Thirteen.)

A Writing Evaluation Form is provided for your use in evaluating your students' writing.

WRITING ASSIGNMENT #2 - *Mythology*

PROMPT

Jason, Perseus, Theseus, Hercules, Odysseus, and Aeneas all made heroic journeys. Odysseus retold his in great detail. Your assignment is to make a travelogue. A travelogue is a journal that describes your journey. If you have been on a vacation, tell all about that. If you have never been on a trip or don't want to tell about a vacation you have had, write about a vacation trip you think you would like to take.

The point of the assignment is for you to practice writing vividly, describing the trip so the reader will enjoy it. Your travelogue should be 500 - 700 words long. You may use photos, magazine pictures, or drawings.

PRE-WRITING

Make a list of places you have been, or places you would like to go. Select one to write about. Make another list of everything you know about that place. Be sure to include adjectives that describe the place and adjectives to describe your feelings about the place. If you are writing about a place you have been, add details about when you went there, and with whom you traveled. Think about whether or not the trip changed you, and how.

You need to make a few basic decisions: Are you going to have any drawings or pictures with your travelogue? Where will they go? How long will you make the travelogue? Once you have made these decisions, write a rough draft of your travelogue.

DRAFTING

In your introductory paragraph, tell who you are, where you went, and why you went there. In the body of the travelogue, describe in detail the things you saw and the people you met. Also include your feelings and reactions about your journey. You should have a concluding paragraph that restates where you went, and summarizes your feelings about the trip.

PROMPT

After you have finished a rough draft of your travelogue, revise it yourself until you are happy with your work. Then, ask a student who sits near you to read your work and tell you what he/she likes best about it, and what things could be improved. Take another look at your travelogue, keeping in mind your critic's suggestions, and make the revisions you feel are necessary.

PROOFREADING

Do a final proofreading of your paper, double checking your grammar, spelling, organization and the clarity of your ideas.

WRITING EVALUATION FORM - *Mythology*

Name_____Date_____Class_____

Writing Assignment #2 for *Mythology*

Circle One For Each Item:

Introduction	excellent	good	fair	poor
Body Paragraphs	excellent	good	fair	poor
Summary	excellent	good	fair	poor
Grammar	excellent	good	fair	poor
Spelling	excellent	good	fair	poor (errors noted)
Punctuation	excellent	good	fair	poor (errors noted)
Legibility	excellent	good	fair	poor (errors noted)

Strengths:

Weaknesses:

Comments/Suggestions:

LESSON TWELVE - *Mythology*

Objectives
1. To do the pre-reading work for Part Five, Chapters 17, 18, & 19
2. To read silently
3. To compose a brief (two to three minute) summary of the reading assignment
4. To practice giving short oral reports to an audience
5. To discuss the main ideas and details in Part Five, Chapters 17, 18, & 19

Activity #1

Have students work independently to complete the pre-reading work for Chapters 17-19.

Activity #2

Since these chapters are composed of short tales, this would be a good time to have the students practice summarizing and giving short oral reports to the class. Assign each short story to one or two students. Have them read the story and prepare a two or three minute summary to tell the class. Remind students that in a summary like this, they should concentrate on retelling the main idea and the most important details.

Activity #3

Invite students to come to the front of the room to give their reports. You may want to allow them to use their notes. Depending on your class, you may want to organize the session as a news broadcast. Students giving the reports could be the news reporters. Have a "news desk" in the front of the room where students can sit and report. Since one of the objectives here is to be brief, assign a student to time the presentations. Students who are not finished when their time is up should stop anyway. You may want to help them rewrite and condense their summaries at another time.

Activity #4

Suggest that students keep a copy of their study guide questions open and take notes during the oral reports. Most of the study guide questions will probably be answered as the students give their presentations. You can quickly answer any remaining questions after the reports are finished.

LESSON THIRTEEN - *Mythology*

Objectives
1. To give students the opportunity to practice their writing skills
2. To give the teacher the opportunity to evaluate students' writing skills

Activity #1
Give students this class period to work on Writing Assignment #2. You may want to let them conference quietly, to brainstorm ideas and serve as peer editors.

Activity #2
Hold brief individual conferences with students about their writing assignment. Use the Writing Evaluation Form presented in Lesson Eleven. Allow students a few days to revise their papers. I suggest grading the revisions on an A-C-E scale (all revisions well done, some revisions made, or no revisions made.) This will speed your grading time and still give some credit for the students' efforts. Assign the due date for the assignment.

LESSON FOURTEEN - *Mythology*

Objectives
1. To do the pre-reading work for Part Six, Chapters 20 & 21
2. To practice reading aloud to an audience
3. To discuss the main ideas and details in Chapters 20 & 21

Activity #1
Have students complete the pre-reading work for this section.

Activity #2
Since these chapters contain very short accounts of many myths, this would be a good place to have students practice their oral reading. Assign a story to each student. Give them time to practice reading silently before they read aloud. Have each student read his or her story aloud to the class. Encourage students to stand in the front of the room to read. Provide a lectern or podium if possible. If necessary, model proper posture, vocal intonation, and audience awareness. If you run out of time for this activity, you may want to extend it for another day.

LESSON FIFTEEN - *Mythology*

Objective
> To write a persuasive argument paper

Activity #1
> Ask students if they have ever been persuaded to do something. Discuss the methods the persuader used. Read a few examples of persuasive writing aloud to the students. Discuss the ways that persuasive writing differs from other types of writing. Make a list of words or phrases that are often used in persuasive writing, and post it somewhere in the room.

Activity #2
> Distribute copies of Writing Assignment #3. Allow students to work on the assignment for the remainder of the class time. Set a due date for the assignment.

WRITING ASSIGNMENT #3 - *Mythology*

PROMPT

Prometheus gave fire to mankind, and then tricked Zeus into accepting the fat and bone as his portion of a sacrifice. In addition, Prometheus knew who would be the mother of the son who would someday dethrone him. Zeus was angry at Prometheus for all of these reasons, and decided to punish him. Zeus had Prometheus bound to a rock. Every day an eagle would come down and eat Prometheus' liver. The liver would grow back, and the eagle would repeat his feast. This was to go on for eternity.

In this writing assignment, Prometheus is entitled to a trial by a jury of the gods before he is convicted and sentenced. You are to act either as the defense (for Prometheus) or the prosecution (against Prometheus.) Your assignment is to write a closing argument to the jury. (This is a lawyer's final summary of his/her case and the best efforts at persuading the jury to his/her side.)

PRE-WRITING

To begin, decide which side you want to take--the defense or the prosecution. On a piece of paper, jot down the main points, the facts which will support your case. Decide which points are your strongest and which of the arguments you will make are weaker. Organize your points from weakest to strongest and jot down anything you can think of which will support or explain your points.

DRAFTING

Begin with an introductory paragraph in which you introduce the jury to your side of the case. Follow that with one paragraph for each of the main points you have to support your case.
Fill in each paragraph with examples and facts which support your main point. Then, write a paragraph in which you make your final closing statements.

PROMPT

When you finish the rough draft of your paper, ask a student who sits near you to read it. After reading your rough draft, he/she should tell you what he/she liked best about your work, which parts were difficult to understand, and ways in which your work could be improved. Re-read your paper considering your critic's comments, and make the corrections you think are necessary.

PROOFREADING

Do a final proofreading of your paper double-checking your grammar, spelling, organization, and the clarity of your ideas.

LESSON SIXTEEN - *Mythology*

Objectives
1. To complete the pe-reading work for Part Seven, Introduction and Chapters 22 & 2
2. To read (silently or orally) Part Seven, Introduction and Chapters 22 & 23
3. To discuss the main ideas and details in Part Seven, Introduction and Chapters 22 & 23

Activity #1
Have students complete the pre-reading work for Part Seven.

Activity #2
Before students start reading, locate the Nordic countries on a map. You may want to repeat the activity from Lesson One, and do a KWL specifically for Norse Mythology. (You can use the same form as in Lesson One.)

Activity #3
Depending on the needs and abilities of your students, have them complete the reading silently, or quietly read aloud with a partner.

Activity #4
Use some of the Short Answer Study Guide Questions as an open-book quiz. Complete the answers to the rest of the questions with the class.

LESSON SEVENTEEN - *Mythology*

Objective
To study in more detail some of the main characters in *Mythology*

Activity #1
Divide your class into ten groups, one for each of the following:
1. Zeus
2. Hera
3. Demeter
4. Dionysus
5. Jason
6. Theseus
7. Perseus
8. Hector
9. Odysseus
10. Sigurd

**You could also use any of the other deities or heroes who are described sufficiently to allow students to successfully complete the assignment.

Each group should write down the characteristics of the character they are assigned. Then they should confer and form an opinion about that character.

Activity #2
Have a spokesperson from each group report the group's findings. Encourage the rest of the class to ask questions. If they disagree with the opinions of the reporting group, they must present evidence from the book to support their argument.
You may want to have a large piece of paper on the chalkboard or bulletin board. Put the name of each of the characters at the top of the chart. Have a writer from each group record the characteristics of the group. Students with artistic ability could draw their interpretations of what the characters look like.

LESSON EIGHTEEN - *Mythology*

Objective
To discuss *Mythology* on a deeper than "direct recall" level
Activity
Discuss the extra questions provided with this packet by having students read or summarize their Writing Assignment #1 papers. Each student should give an answer to the question he worked on for his paper. Use these "reports" as a springboard for discussion of each question.
Write the "answers" to the questions on the board (or overhead projector transparency) for students to copy for study use. (Or you could just allow students to take notes and then show a transparency at the end of the discussions as a brief review so students can check their notes.)
Collect each student's writing assignment after he finishes his oral presentation.

LESSON NINETEEN - *Mythology*

Objectives
    1. To widen the breadth of students' knowledge about the topics discussed or touched upon in *Mythology*

    2. To check students' non-fiction assignments.

Activity

    Ask each student to give a brief oral report about the nonfiction work he/she read for the nonfiction assignment. Your criteria for evaluating this report will vary depending on the level of your students. You may wish for students to give a complete report without using notes of any kind, or you may want students to read directly from a written report, or you may want to do something in between these two extremes. Just make students aware of your criteria in ample time for them to prepare their reports.

    Start with one student's report. After that, ask if anyone else in the class has read on a topic related to the first student's report. If no on has, choose another student at random. After each report, be sure to ask if anyone has a report related to the one just completed. That will help keep a continuity during the discussion of the reports.

LESSON TWENTY - *Mythology*

Objective
    To review all of the vocabulary work done in this unit

Activity

    Choose one (or more) of the following vocabulary review activities and spend your class period as directed in the activity. Some of the materials for these review activities are located in the Extra Activities Packet in this unit.

VOCABULARY REVIEW ACTIVITIES

1. Divide your class into two teams and have an old-fashioned spelling or definition bee.

2. Give each of your students (or students in groups of two, three or four) a *Mythology* Vocabulary Word Search Puzzle. The first person (group) to find all of the vocabulary words in the puzzle wins.

3. Give students a *Mythology* Vocabulary Word Search Puzzle without the word list. The person or group to find the most vocabulary words in the puzzle wins.

4. Use a *Mythology* Vocabulary Crossword Puzzle. Put the puzzle onto a transparency on the overhead projector (so everyone can see it), and do the puzzle together as a class.

5. Give students a *Mythology* Vocabulary Matching Worksheet to do.

6. Divide your class into two teams. Use the *Mythology* vocabulary words with their letters jumbled as a word list. Student 1 from Team A faces off against Student 1 from Team B. You write the first jumbled word on the board. The first student (1A or 1B) to unscramble the word wins the chance for his/her team to score points. If 1A wins the jumble, go to student 2A and give him/her a definition. He/she must give you the correct spelling of the vocabulary word which fits that definition. If he/she does, Team A scores a point, and you give student 3A a definition for which you expect a correctly spelled matching vocabulary word. Continue giving Team A definitions until some team member makes an incorrect response. An incorrect response sends the game back to the jumbled-word face off, this time with students 2A and 2B. Instead of repeating giving definitions to the first few students of each team, continue with the student after the one who gave the last incorrect response on the team. For example, if Team B wins the jumbled-word face-off, and student 5B gave the last incorrect answer for Team B, you would start this round of definition questions with student 6B, and so on. The team with the most points wins!

7. Have students write a story in which they correctly use as many vocabulary words as possible. Have students read their compositions orally. Post the most original compositions on your bulletin board.

LESSON TWENTY-ONE - *Mythology*

Objective
    To review the main ideas presented in *Mythology*

Activity #1
    Choose one of the review games/activities included in the packet and spend your class period as outlined there.

Activity #2
    Remind students of the date for the Unit Test. Stress the review of the Study Guides and their class notes as a last minute, brush-up review for homework.

REVIEW GAMES/ACTIVITIES

1. Ask the class to make up a unit test for *Mythology*. The test should have 4 sections: multiple choice, true/false, short answer and essay. Students may use ½ period to make the test, including a separate answer sheet, and then swap papers and use the other ½ class period to take a test a classmate has devised. (Open book)

2. Take ½ period for students to make up true and false questions (including the answers). Collect the papers and divide the class into two teams. Draw a big tic-tac-toe board on the chalk board. Make one team X and one team O. Ask questions to each side, giving each student one turn. If the question is answered correctly, that student's team's letter (X or O) is placed in the box. If the answer is incorrect, no mark is placed in the box. The object is to get three marks in a row like tic-tac-toe. You may want to keep track of the number of games won for each team.

3. Take ½ period for students to make up questions (true/false and short answer). Collect the questions. Divide the class into two teams. You'll alternate asking questions to individual members of teams A & B (like a spelling bee). The question keeps going from A to B until it is correctly answered, then a new question is asked. A correct answer does not allow the team to get another question. Correct answers are +2 points; incorrect answers are -1 point.

4. Allow students time to quiz each other (in pairs) from their study guides and class notes.

5. Give students a *Mythology* crossword puzzle to complete.

LESSON TWENTY-ONE - *Mythology* continued

REVIEW GAMES/ACTIVITIES

6. Divide your class into two teams. Use the *Mythology* crossword words with their letters jumbled as a word list. Student 1 from Team A faces off against Student 1 from Team B. You write the first jumbled word on the board. The first student (1A or 1B) to unscramble the word wins the chance for his/her team to score points. If 1A wins the jumble, go to student 2A and give him/her a clue. He/she must give you the correct word which matches that clue. If he/she does, Team A scores a point, and you give student 3A a clue for which you expect another correct response. Continue giving Team A clues until some team member makes an incorrect response. An incorrect response sends the game back to the jumbled-word face off, this time with students 2A and 2B. Instead of repeating giving clues to the first few students of each team, continue with the student after the one who gave the last incorrect response on the team.

7. Take on the persona of "The Answer Person." Allow students to ask any question about the book. Answer the questions, or tell students where to look in the book to find the answer.

8. Students may enjoy playing charades with events from the story. Select a student to start. Give him/her a card with a scene or event from the story. Allow the players to use their books to find the scene being described. The first person to guess each charade performs the next one.

9. Play a categories-type quiz game. Make an overhead transparency of the categories form. Divide the class into teams of three or four players each. Have each team choose a recorder and a banker. Choose a team to go first. That team will choose a category and point amount. Ask the question to the entire class. (Use the Study Guide Quiz and Vocabulary questions.) Give the teams one minute to discuss the answer and write it down. Walk around the room and check the answers. Each team that answers correctly receives the points. (Incorrect answers are not penalized; they just don't receive any point.) Cross out that square on the playing board. Play continues until all squares have been used. The winning team is the one with the most points. You can assign bonus points to any square or squares you choose.

10. Have students complete the last column (What I Learned) of the KWL sheet you distributed in Lesson One. Discuss their answers with the class.

NOTE: If students do not need the extra review, omit this lesson and go on to the test.

QUIZ GAME *Mythology*

Vocabulary	Parts One & Two	Parts Three & Four	Parts Five & Six	Part Seven
100	100	100	100	100
200	200	200	200	200
300	300	300	300	300
400	400	400	400	400
500	500	500	500	500

LESSON TWENTY-TWO - *Mythology*

Objective

To test students' understanding of the main ideas and themes in *Mythology*.

Activity #1

Distribute the *Mythology* Unit Tests. Go over the instructions in detail and allow the students the entire class period to complete the exam.

Activity #2

Collect all test papers and assigned books prior to the end of the class period.

NOTES ABOUT THE UNIT TESTS IN THIS UNIT:

There are 5 different unit tests which follow.

There are two short answer tests which are based primarily on facts from the novel. The answer key short answer unit test 1 follows the student test. The answer key for short answer test 2 follows the student short answer unit test 2.

There is one advanced short answer unit test. It is based on the extra discussion questions. Use the matching key for short answer unit test 2 to check the matching section of the advanced short answer unit test. There is no key for the short answer questions. The answers will be based on the discussions you have had during class.

There are two multiple choice unit tests. Following the two unit tests, you will find an answer sheet on which students should mark their answers. The same answer sheet should be used for both tests; however, students' answers will be different for each test. Following the students' answer sheet for the multiple choice tests you will find your answer keys.

The short answer tests have a vocabulary section. You should choose 10 of the vocabulary words from this unit, read them orally and have the students write them down. Then, either have students write a definition or use the words in sentences.

UNIT TESTS

SHORT ANSWER UNIT TEST 1 - *Mythology*

I. Matching

____ 1. Zeus   A. took the Argo in quest of the Golden Fleece

____ 2. Dionysus   B. rescued Brynhild from Ring of Fire

____ 3. Jason   C. Jupiter; master of the thunderbolt

____ 4. Helen   D. Norse God of Love and Beauty

____ 5. Hera   E. took ten years to get home after Trojan War

____ 6. Odysseus   F. Norse god who searched for wisdom

____ 7. Poseidon   G. Neptune; ruler of the sea

____ 8. Odin   H. Juno; wife of Zeus, patron of marriage

____ 9. Sigurd   I. God of Wine; center of belief in immortality

____ 10. Freya   J. wife of Menelaus, kidnapped by Trojans

II. Short Answer

1. Define mythology. What do Greek and Roman mythology show us about the human race of long ago?

2. Briefly describe the characteristics and functions of any two of the following gods and goddesses: Athena, Phoebus Apollo, Artemis, or Aphrodite.

Short Answer Unit Test 1 - *Mythology* continued

3. Briefly retell the story of Demeter (Ceres).

4. Briefly describe the Greek idea of the way the world and mankind were created.

5. What was the Golden Fleece, and why did Jason undertake the search for it?

6. Why did Hercules perform his twelve labors?

Short Answer Unit Test 1 - *Mythology* continued

7. What was the cause of the Trojan War?

8. Briefly retell the story of Oedipus.

9. What was the choice the Norse hero made, and why did he make it?

10. What, according to Hamilton, were the Norsemen's two characteristics?

Short Answer Unit Test 1 - *Mythology* continued

III. Essay

Choose any one of the following myths, and retell it in detail. Then discuss the element of nature, or lesson for mankind, that is being explained in the myth.

    1) Pandora
    2) Prometheus
    3) Pegasus and Bellerophon
    4) Odysseus
    5) Hercules

Short Answer Unit Test 1 - *Mythology* continued

IV. Vocabulary

Listen to the words and write them down. Go back and write in the correct definition for each.

1.

2.

3.

4.

5.

6.

7.

8.

9.

10.

ANSWER KEY SHORT ANSWER UNIT TEST 1 - *Mythology*

I. Matching

C.	1. Zeus	A.	took the Argo in quest of the Golden Fleece
I.	2. Dionysus	B.	rescued Brynhild from Ring of Fire
A.	3. Jason	C.	Jupiter; master of the thunderbolt
J.	4. Helen	D.	Norse God of Love and Beauty
H.	5. Hera	E.	took ten years to get home after Trojan War
E.	6. Odysseus	F.	Norse god who searched for wisdom
G.	7. Poseidon	G.	Neptune; ruler of the sea
F.	8. Odin	H.	Juno; wife of Zeus, patron of marriage
B.	9. Sigurd	I.	God of Wine; center of belief in immortality
D.	10. Freya	J.	wife of Menelaus, kidnapped by Trojans

II. Short Answer

1. Define mythology. What do Greek and Roman mythology show us about the human race of long ago?

   Mythology is a collection of stories about the origin and history of a people and their gods and heroes. It incorporates elements of science, literature, and religion. Myths often explain something in nature. Greek and Roman mythology shows us the way the human race thought and felt. It was an attempt to turn a fearful world into one of beauty.

2. Describe the characteristics and functions of any two of the following gods and goddesses: Athena, Phoebus Apollo, Artemis, or Aphrodite.

   Athena sprang full grown from the head of Zeus. She was the protector of civilized life. She invented the bridle, and was the first to tame hoses for men's use. She was known as the Maiden, or Parthenos, and her temple was the Parthenon. Athena symbolized wisdom, reason, and purity. Phoebus Apollo played the golden lyre, and was also the Archer and Healer. His oracle at Delphi was a direct link between gods and men. Artemis (Diana) was the Huntsman. Aphrodite (Venus) was the Goddess of Love and Beauty.

3. Retell the story of Demeter (Ceres.)

   Demeter was the Goddess of the Corn. Her daughter, Persephone, was carried off to the underworld by Hades. Demeter was greatly upset, and no crops grew on the earth. Zeus then ruled that Persephone would spend four months of every year in the underworld, and the rest of the time on the earth with her mother. The crops grew and flowers bloomed while Persephone was on the earth, but all died when she went to the underworld.

4. Describe the Greek idea of the way the world and mankind were created.

   They thought Chaos, or formless confusion, was at the very beginning. Night and Erebus, the children of Chaos, were created next. They created Love, who created Light and Day, and then Earth was created. Mother Earth and Father Heaven then had their monster children, including the Cyclopes, and the Titans. Cronus (Saturn), one of the Titans, killed his father and became ruler. The Giants and Erinyes (Furies) sprang from his father's blood. The gods were the children of Cronus and Rhea (Ops), his sister-queen. The gods then created mankind.

5. What was the Golden Fleece, and why did Jason undertake the search for it?

   Hermes had sent a golden ram to save a young prince, Phrixus, from being sacrificed at the altar. Later, Phrixus sacrificed the ram to Zeus and gave the Golden Fleece to King Aeetes. Jason was trying to regain the kingdom that had been taken from his father by a cousin. The cousin agreed to give it back if Jason could bring him the Golden Fleece. Jason loved adventure, and set off in his ship, the *Argo,* to find the Fleece.

6. Why did Hercules perform his twelve labors?

   Hera had made him mad. He killed his wife and children. When he came out of his madness he wanted to do penance for his deeds. His cousin, King Eurystheus, gave him the twelve labors.

7. What was the cause of the Trojan War?

   Aphrodite took Paris to the most beautiful woman in the world. She was Helen, who lived in Greece and was married to King Menelaus of Sparta. Paris took her back to Troy with him. All of Helen's former suitors allied with Menelaus to get her back. This was the start of the Trojan War.

8. Retell the story of Oedipus.

   Oedipus was the son of King Laius and Jocasta, of Thebes. Apollo had declared that Oedipus was destined to kill his father, so he was set on a mountain top while a baby to die. He was rescued and raised by King Polybus of Corinth. As an adult, Oedipus also heard the prophecy of the oracle. Since he believed he was the son of King Polybus, he left Corinth so that the prophecy would not come true. On his way to Thebes he killed some other travelers, not realizing that Laius, his real father, was one of the men he had killed. He then arrived in Thebes and saved the city from the terrorism of the Sphinx. Oedipus married Laius' widow and his own mother, Jocasta. When she learned the truth, she killed herself. Then Oedipus blinded himself and went into exile until he died.

9. What was the choice the Norse hero made, and why did he make it?

   The Norsemen believed that it was a hopeless cause for the forces of good to fight to defend against the forces of evil. However, they still fought, because they believed a brave death would entitle them to a seat in Valhalla. They believed that heroism was the one good that man could attain, and that the proof of a hero was death. The power of good was shown by constantly resisting evil in the face of defeat. The Norse hero chose between yielding to evil or dying for good.

10. What, according to Hamilton, were the Norsemen's two characteristics?
    They were heroic and had common sense.

SHORT ANSWER UNIT TEST 2 - *Mythology*

I. Matching

____ 1. Hera

____ 2. Odin

____ 3. Dionysus

____ 4. Sigurd

____ 5. Poseidon

____ 6. Zeus

____ 7. Freya

____ 8. Helen

____ 9. Odysseus

____ 10. Jason

A. took ten years to get home after the Trojan War

B. Norse god who searched for wisdom

C. Neptune; ruler of the sea

D. took the *Argo* in quest of the Golden Fleece

E. Norse Goddess of Love and Beauty

F. Juno; wife of Zeus, patron of marriage

G. rescued Brynhild from Ring of Fire

H. wife of Menelaus, kidnapped by Trojans

I. God of Wine, center of belief in immortality

J. Jupiter; master of the thunderbolt

II. Short Answer

1. Who were the first parents, and who were their children and grandchildren?

2. Briefly describe the characteristics and functions of any two of the following gods and goddesses: Hephaestus, Hestia, Cupid, Ares, or The Muses and Graces.

Short Answer Unit Test 2 - *Mythology* continued

3. What were the two central ideas in the worship of Dionysus, and why did Dionysus become the center of the belief in immortality?

4. How did Zeus become the ruler of heaven and earth?

5. Why did Zeus punish Prometheus, and how did he do this?

6. Describe three of the twelve labors of Hercules.

Short Answer Unit Test 2 - *Mythology* continued

7. What was the Judgment of Paris, and why was it significant?

8. Briefly retell the story of Odysseus.

9. Briefly retell the story of Signy and Sigmund.

10. Which days of the week were named after Norse gods?

Short Answer Unit Test 2 - *Mythology* continued

III. Essay

Choose any one of the following myths, and retell it in detail. Then discuss the element of nature, or lesson for mankind, that is being explained in the myth.

    1) Sigurd
    2) Demeter and Persephone
    3) Theseus
    4) The House of Atreus
    5) Aeneas

Short Answer Unit Test 2 - *Mythology* continued

V. Vocabulary

Listen to the vocabulary words and spell them. After you have spelled all the words, go back and write down the definitions.

1.

2.

3.

4.

5.

6.

7.

8.

9.

10.

ANSWER KEY SHORT ANSWER UNIT TEST 2 - *Mythology*

Use this answer key for the matching tests in Short Answer Unit Test 2 and the Advanced Short Answer Test.

I. Matching

F. 1. Hera   A. took ten years to get home after Trojan War

B. 2. Odin   B. Norse god who searched for wisdom

I. 3. Dionysus   C. Neptune; ruler of the sea

G. 4. Sigurd   D. took the *Argo* in quest of the Golden Fleece

C. 5. Poseidon   E. Norse Goddess of Love and Beauty

J. 6. Zeus   F. Juno; wife of Zeus, patron of marriage

E. 7. Freya   G. rescued Brynhild from Ring of Fire

H. 8. Helen   H. wife of Menelaus, kidnapped by Trojans

A. 9. Odysseus   I. God of Wine, center of belief in immortality

D. 10. Jason   J. Jupiter; master of the thunderbolt

II. Short Answer

1. Who were the first parents, and who were their children and grandchildren?
    Heaven and Earth were the first parents. The Titans (Cronus-Saturn, Ocean, Tethys, Hyperion, Mnemosyne, Themis, and Iapetus,) were their children, the gods were their grandchildren.

2. Briefly describe the characteristics and functions of any two of the following gods and goddesses; Hephaestus, Hestia, Cupid, Ares, or The Muses and Graces.
    Hephaestus (Vulcan) was the God of Fire. He made the armor and furniture for the gods. He was also the patron of handicrafts and the protector of smiths.
    Hestia (Vesta) was Zeus' sister and the Goddess of the Hearth. She does not play an important part in the myths, although offerings were made to her in all homes.
    Cupid (Eros) was the God of Love. The later poets said he was Aphrodite's son.
    Ares (Mars) was the God of War.
    There were nine Muses, the daughters of Zeus and Memory. They were known for their

singing, and each had a special field. There were three Graces: Splendor, Mirth, and Good Cheer. They were always together.

3. What were the two central ideas in the worship of Dionysus, and why did Dionysus become the center of the belief in immortality?

    Dionysus was the god of the Vine. He could give either joy or savage brutality, because wine could be both bad and good. He was the symbol of the vine, which is pruned every year, and then grows back in the spring. His followers believed that his death and resurrection indicate the eternal life of the soul.

4. How did Zeus become the ruler of heaven and earth?

    His mother, Rhea, hid Zeus from Cronus when he was born. When Zeus was grown he forced Cronus to disgorge his five siblings. Zeus and his brothers warred against Cronus and the Titans. Zeus eventually mastered the use of thunder and lightning, his brother and sister gods became more powerful, and they defeated Cronus and the Titans.

5. Why did Zeus punish Prometheus, and how did he do this?

    Prometheus had stolen fire for mankind, and had also arranged for them to receive the best part of any sacrificial animals. Prometheus was also the only one who knew who would be the mother of the son who would dethrone Zeus. Zeus had his servants, Force and Violence, bind Prometheus to a rock. Every day an eagle would come down and eat Prometheus' liver. Prometheus never gave in, but he was eventually released.

6. Describe three of the twelve labors of Hercules.

    (TEACHERS, ALL LABORS ARE SUMMARIZED HERE FOR YOU.)

    1) He killed the lion of Nemea by choking it.
    2) He killed the nine-headed Hydra.
    3) He brought back alive a stag with golden horns.
    4) He captured a great boar.
    5) He cleaned the very dirty Augean stables by diverting two rivers and making them flood the stables.
    6) He shot the birds that plagued the people of Stymphalus.
    7) He took a bull that belonged to Minos of Crete.
    8) He killed King Diomedes, and took his man-eating mares.
    9) He stole the girdle of Hippolyta, Queen of the Amazons. He killed her in the process.
    10) He brought back the cattle of Geryon.
    11) He brought back the Golden Apples of the Hesperides. He held the vault of heaven for Atlas so that Atlas could find the apples for him. Then he tricked Atlas into taking the heavens back onto his own shoulders.
    12) He went to the underworld and freed Theseus from the Chair of Forgetfulness.

7. What was the Judgment of Paris, and why was it significant?

   Paris was the son of King Priam of Troy. The goddesses Hera, Aphrodite, and Pallas Athena were feuding over who was the fairest, and would become the owner of the golden apple. They asked Paris to listen to each of their bribes and choose who would get the apple. He liked Aphrodite's bribe, that the fairest woman in the world would be his. He awarded her the Golden Apple. Aphrodite took Paris to Helen, the most beautiful woman in the world. She lived in Greece and was married to King Menelaus of Sparta. Paris took her back to Troy with him. All of Helen's former suitors allied with Menelaus to get her back. This was the start of the Trojan War.

8. Briefly retell the story of Odysseus.

   Odysseus was one of the Greek heroes of the Trojan War. The Greeks took a prophetess out of Athena's temple in Troy, and made Athena furious at this sacrilege. She asked Poseidon to help her take revenge on the Greeks. Poseidon caused a great tempest in the sea that drowned many of the Greeks. Odysseus was shipwrecked. He suffered through ten years of wandering, which he related to King Alcinous of Phaeacia when he finally arrived there. Odysseus and his men encountered the Lotus-Eaters, whose food made men forget their desire to go home. They then met the Cyclops, Polyphemus, who devoured several of Odysseus' men. Odysseus and the remainder of his men put out the Cyclops' eye and escaped. When they reached the nymph Circe's island, she turned the men into swine. Hermes helped Odysseus resist her powers, and she was so impressed that she released his men and treated them as her guests. Next Odysseus traveled to Hades to find the spirit of the prophet Teiresias, and then follow his directions. Then he and his men passed the island of the Sirens, whose songs enticed men. Odysseus had himself tied to the ship's mast, and plugged the ears of his men with wax so they could not hear the songs. They safely got through the passage between Scylla and Charybdis. When they arrived at the Island of the Sun, some of the men killed his oxen. As a punishment, the sun drowned all but Odysseus. He drifted to the island of Calypso, where he lived for many years. At last Athena sent Hermes to tell Calypso to let Odysseus go home. On his way home he was set upon by Poseidon, and finally arrived at the country of the Phaeacians. After Odysseus related his story to King Alcinous, the king gave him a ship. The other men gave him presents and provisions. When he returned home, he discovered that many men had been courting his wife, Penelope. She was doing her best to avoid marrying any of them. The suitors were rude and were eating all of her food, but she still held out hope that her husband would return. He used his bow and, with the help of his son, Telemachus, and a servant, Eumaeus, killed all of the suitors.

9. Briefly retell the story of Signy and Sigmund.

   They were brother and sister. Signy's husband killed her father and all of her brothers except Sigurd. She disguised herself, visited him, and conceived a son, Sinfiotli. She later sent the boy to live with Sigmund. Sigmund and Sinfiotli killed Signy's husband and children in retaliation. Then she killed herself.

10. Which days of the week were named after Norse gods?

    Thursday was named for Thor, the Thunder God. Wednesday was named for Odin, which was Woden in the south. Tuesday was named for Tyr, the god of War, and Friday was named for Freya, the Goddess of Love and Beauty.

ADVANCED SHORT ANSWER TEST - *Mythology*

I. Matching

_____ 1. Hera   A. took ten years to get home after Trojan War

_____ 2. Odin   B. Norse god who searched for wisdom

_____ 3. Dionysus   C. Neptune; ruler of the sea

_____ 4. Sigurd   D. took the *Argo* in quest of the Golden Fleece

_____ 5. Poseidon   E. Norse Goddess of Love and Beauty

_____ 6. Zeus   F. Juno; wife of Zeus, patron of marriage

_____ 7. Freya   G. rescued Brynhild from Ring of Fire

_____ 8. Helen   H. Wife of Menelaus, kidnapped by Trojans

_____ 9. Odysseus   I. God of Wine, center of belief in immortality

_____ 10. Jason   J. Jupiter; master of the thunderbolt

II. Short Answer

1. Discuss the changes in the persona of Zeus over the course of the myths.

2. What influence did the religion of Dionysus have on later religions?

Advanced Short Answer Test - *Mythology* continued

3. Several of the myths explain something in nature. Choose one of these myths. Summarize it. and tell what natural event is being explained.

4. Compare and contrast the gods of the Greek/Roman myths with those of the Norse myths.

5. Compare and contrast the creation myths of the Greek/Roman and Norsemen.

Advanced Short Answer Test - *Mythology* continued

III. Actions and Consequences. Each of the following characters acted in a way to bring about a direct consequence. Summarize each character's actions and the consequences.

1. Tantalus

2. Prometheus

3. Atlas

4. Atalanta

5. Signy

MULTIPLE CHOICE UNIT TEST 1 - *Mythology*

I. Matching

1. Zeus
2. Dionysus
3. Jason
4. Helen
5. Hera
6. Odysseus
7. Poseidon
8. Odin
9. Sigurd
10. Freya

A. took the *Argo* in quest of the Golden Fleece
B. rescued Brynhild from Ring of Fire
C. Jupiter; master of the thunderbolt
D. Norse God of Love and Beauty
E. took ten years to get home after Trojan War
F. Norse god who searched for wisdom
G. Neptune; ruler of the sea
H. Juno; wife of Zeus, patron of marriage
I. God of Wine; center of belief in immortality
J. Wife of Menelaus, kidnapped by Trojans

II. Multiple Choice

1. True or False: The myths have elements of science, literature, and religion.
    A. True
    B. False

2. Which of the following statement is **not** correct?
    A. Phoebus Apollo played the golden lyre, and was also the Archer and Healer. His oracle at Delphi was a direct link between gods and men.
    B. Athena was known as "the goddess with three forms;" Selene in the sky, Athena on earth, and Hecate in the underworld.
    C. Artemis was the Huntsman in Chief and the protector of youth and wildlife.
    D. Aphrodite was the Goddess of Love and Beauty.

3. Whose story is told here? She was the Goddess of the Corn. Her daughter was carried off to the underworld by Hades. The mother was greatly upset, and no crops grew on the earth. Zeus then ruled that the daughter would spend four months of every year in the underworld, and the rest of the time on the earth with her mother. The crops grew and flowers bloomed while the daughter was on the earth, but all died when she went to the underworld.
    A. Demeter was the mother and Persephone was daughter.
    B. Ceres was the mother and Phoebe was the daughter.
    C. Persephone was the mother and Doria was the daughter.
    D. Rhea was the mother and Demeter was the daughter.

4. What did the Greeks think was at the very beginning of things?
    A. They thought Cosmos, or a mix of everything, was at the beginning.
    B. They thought it was Water, the gift of Life.
    C. They thought it was Eternity.
    D. They thought Chaos, or formless confusion, was at the beginning.

Multiple Choice Unit Test 1 - *Mythology* continued

5. Why was Jason's journey significant?
    A. It was the first journey ever made over land instead of water.
    B. It was the first journey that was ever recorded.
    C. Jason was the first hero in Europe who went on a great journey.
    D. Jason made the first map while on his journey.

6. Why did Hercules perform his twelve labors?
    A. He was doing penance for killing his wife and children.
    B. Theseus challenged him to see who the greatest hero in Greece was.
    C. Zeus had told Hercules that if he could perform all of the labors successfully, he would be given immortality and a place among the gods.
    D. He had to do them before he could marry the woman he loved.

7. What was the cause of the Trojan War?
    A. The Trojans killed Tyndareus and the Greeks sought revenge.
    B. The Greeks wanted to establish trade routes through Troy, but the Trojans refused.
    C. The King of Troy had a vision from Athena that he was destined to conquer Greece, and he acted on the dream.
    D. Paris kidnapped Helen, the Greek wife of King Menelaus of Sparta. All of Helen's former suitors allied with Menelaus to get her back.

8. What wrong did Oedipus commit?
    A. He stole the necklace that Hephaestus had given his mother and gave it to Hera as a present.
    B. He killed the great serpent that had been protecting the city of Thebes.
    C. He killed his father, King Laius, and married his mother, Jocasta.
    D. He gave military secrets to the Trojans.

9. What was the choice the Norse hero made?
    A. The Norse hero chose between staying and fighting on earth or having a pleasant life in Asgard.
    B. The Norse hero really had no choice; the gods had already chosen him as a hero.
    C. The Norse hero had to choose a god to serve as his protector. If, for some reason, he fell out of favor with that god, none of the others would help him.
    D. The Norse hero chose between yielding to evil or dying for good.

10. What, according to Hamilton, were the Norsemen's two characteristics?
    A. They were strong but not very bright.
    B. They were heroic and had common sense.
    C. They were religious and adventurous.
    D. They were long-suffering and patient.

Multiple Choice Unit Test 1 - *Mythology* continued

III. Matching

1. Sisyphus   A. fell in love with his reflection in a pool

2. Prometheus   B. lost a footrace when distracted by golden apples

3. Narcissus   C. killed by Artemis, placed in the sky as a constellation

4. Pygmalion   D. tried forever to roll a rock uphill

5. Icarus   E. killed herself after family was killed by her brother

6. Hercules   F. bound to a rock; every day an eagle ate his liver

7. Atalanta   G. fell in love with a statue he made

8. Arachne   H. killed his wife and children while in a mad trance

9. Signy   I. weaver turned into a spider by Minerva

10. Orion   J. his wings melted when he flew too close to the sun

Multiple Choice Unit Test 1 - *Mythology* continued

IV. Vocabulary (Matching)

1. promontory
2. somber
3. suffrage
4. atrociously
5. prodigy
6. destitute
7. pestilence
8. circumvent
9. acquittal
10. expiating
11. renown
12. emulate
13. dauntless
14. susceptible
15. disdainful
16. prototype
17. eminently
18. austere
19. plausible
20. torrent

A. making amends, atoning
B. severe, having no decoration
C. outstanding, of high quality
D. horribly, cruelly
E. an original that serves as a model
F. to go around or bypass
G. imitate
H. a person who has exceptional talents or powers
I. a fatal epidemic disease
J. without fear, not intimidated
K. easily affected or influenced
L. fame
M. a high ridge of land that juts out into the water
N. gloomy, depressing
O. a freeing from a charge or accusation
P. the right to vote
Q. impoverished, lacking the means of subsistence
R. having some truth, but still open to doubt
S. a turbulent or overwhelming flow
T. showing contempt

MULTIPLE CHOICE UNIT TEST 2 - *Mythology*

I. Matching

1. Hera
2. Odin
3. Dionysus
4. Sigurd
5. Poseidon
6. Zeus
7. Freya
8. Helen
9. Odysseus
10. Jason

A. Took ten years to get home after the Trojan War
B. Norse god who searched for wisdom
C. Neptune; ruler of the sea
D. Took the *Argo* in quest of the Golden Fleece
E. Norse Goddess of Love and Beauty
F. Juno; wife of Zeus, patron of marriage
G. Rescued Brynhild from Ring of Fire
H. Wife of Menelaus, kidnapped by Trojans
I. God of Wine, center of belief in immortality
J. Jupiter; master of the thunderbolt

II. Multiple Choice

1. What, according to Hamilton, were the Norsemen's two characteristics?
    A. They were strong but not very bright.
    B. They were heroic and had common sense.
    C. They were religious and adventurous
    D. They were long-suffering and patient.

2. Why did Hercules perform his twelve labors?
    A. He was doing penance for killing his wife and children.
    B. Theseus challenged him to see who the greatest hero in Greece was.
    C. Zeus had told Hercules that if he could perform all of the labors successfully, he would be given immortality and a place among the gods.
    D. He had to do them before he could marry the woman he loved.

Multiple Choice Unit Test 2 - *Mythology* continued

3. What was the choice the Norse hero made?
    A. The Norse hero chose between staying and fighting on earth or having a pleasant life in Asgard.
    B. The Norse hero really had no choice; the gods had already chosen him as a hero.
    C. The Norse hero had to choose a god to serve as his protector. If, for some reason, he fell out of favor with that god, none of the others would help him.
    D. The Norse hero chose between yielding to evil or dying for good.

4. True or False: The myths have elements of science, literature, and religion.
    A. True
    B. False

5. What did the Greeks think was at the very beginning of things?
    A. They thought Cosmos, or a mix of everything, was at the beginning.
    B. They thought it was Water, the gift of Life.
    C. They thought it was Eternity.
    D. They thought Chaos, or formless confusion, was at the beginning.

6. What wrong did Oedipus commit?
    A. He stole the necklace that Hephaestus had given his mother and gave it to Hera as a present.
    B. He killed the great serpent that had been protecting the city of Thebes.
    C. He killed his father, King Laius, and married his mother, Jocasta.
    D. He gave military secrets to the Trojans.

7. Why was Jason's journey significant?
    A. It was the first journey ever made over land instead of water.
    B. It was the first journey that was ever recorded.
    C. Jason was the first hero in Europe who went on a great journey.
    D. Jason made the first map while on his journey.

8. Which of the following statement is **not** correct?
    A. Phoebus Apollo played the golden lyre, and was also the Archer and Healer. His oracle at Delphi was a direct link between gods and men.
    B. Athena was known as "the goddess with three forms;" Selene in the sky, Athena on earth, and Hecate in the underworld.
    C. Artemis was the Huntsman in Chief and the protector of youth and wildlife.
    D. Aphrodite was the Goddess of Love and Beauty.

Multiple Choice Unit Test 2 - *Mythology* continued

9. Whose story is told here? She was the Goddess of the Corn. Her daughter was carried off to the underworld by Hades. The mother was greatly upset, and no crops grew on the earth. Zeus then ruled that the daughter would spend four months of every year in the underworld, and the rest of the time on the earth with her mother. The crops grew and flowers bloomed while the daughter was on the earth, but all died when she went to the underworld.
   A. Demeter was the mother and Persephone was daughter.
   B. Ceres was the mother and Phoebe was the daughter.
   C. Persephone was the mother and Doria was the daughter.
   D. Rhea was the mother and Demeter was the daughter.

10. What was the cause of the Trojan War?
    A. The Trojans killed Tyndareus and the Greeks sought revenge.
    B. The Greeks wanted to establish trade routes through Troy, but the Trojans refused.
    C. The King of Troy had a vision from Athena that he was destined to conquer Greece, and he acted on the dream.
    D. Paris kidnapped Helen, the Greek wife of King Menelaus of Sparta. All of Helen's former s suitors allied with Menelaus to get her back.

III. Matching

1. Arachne
2. Atalanta
3. Sisyphus
4. Hercules
5. Icarus
6. Narcissus
7. Orion
8. Prometheus
9. Pygmalion
10. Signy

A. killed by Artemis, placed in the sky as a constellation
B. fell in love with his reflection in a pool
C. lost a footrace when distracted by golden apples
D. weaver turned into a spider by Minerva
E. killed herself after family was killed by her brother
F. his wings melted when he flew too close to the sun
G. tried forever to roll a rock uphill
H. fell in love with a statue he made
I. bound to a rock; every day an eagle ate his liver
J. killed his wife and children while in a mad trance

Multiple Choice Unit Test 2 - *Mythology* continued

IV. Vocabulary (Matching)

1. desolate
2. vindictive
3. sustenance
4. acquiesce
5. unfathomable
6. chagrined
7. implacable
8. exonerate
9. discerning
10. sordid
11. inexorable
12. abashed
13. succored
14. inevitable
15. audacity
16. capricious
17. ludicrous
18. atonement
19. manifest
20. clamor

A. unforgiving, seeking revenge
B. making amends for an injury or wrong
C. embarrassed due to failure or disappointment
D. barren, lifeless
E. daring, boldness
F. loud expression of discontent
G. assisted, helped
H. not able to be understood
I. embarrassed, ashamed
J. clear, understandable
K. distinguishing, perceiving as being different
L. absurd, incongruous
M. the supporting of life or health
N. impulsive, given to whim
O. to consent without protest
P. not able to be persuaded
Q. not able to be appeased
R. impossible to avoid
S. morally degraded
T. to free from blame

ANSWER SHEET - *Mythology*
Multiple Choice Unit Tests

I. Matching

1. ____
2. ____
3. ____
4. ____
5. ____
6. ____
7. ____
8. ____
9. ____
10. ____

II. Multiple Choice

1. (A) (B) (C) (D)
2. (A) (B) (C) (D)
3. (A) (B) (C) (D)
4. (A) (B) (C) (D)
5. (A) (B) (C) (D)
6. (A) (B) (C) (D)
7. (A) (B) (C) (D)
8. (A) (B) (C) (D)
9. (A) (B) (C) (D)
10. (A) (B) (C) (D)

III. Matching

1. ____
2. ____
3. ____
4. ____
5. ____
6. ____
7. ____
8. ____
9. ____
10. ____

IV. Vocabulary

1. ____
2. ____
3. ____
4. ____
5. ____
6. ____
7. ____
8. ____
9. ____
10. ____
11. ____
12. ____
13. ____
14. ____
15. ____
16. ____
17. ____
18. ____
19. ____
20. ____

ANSWER SHEET KEY - *Mythology*
Multiple Choice Unit Test 1

I. Matching
1. C.
2. I.
3. A.
4. J.
5. H.
6. E.
7. G.
8. F.
9. B.
10. D.

II. Multiple Choice
1. (...) (B) (C) (D)
2. (A) (...) (C) (D)
3. (...) (B) (C) (D)
4. (A) (B) (C) (...)
5. (A) (B) (...) (D)
6. (...) B) (C) (D)
7. (A) (B) (C) ...)
8. (A) (B) (...) (D)
9. (A) (B) (C) (...)
10. (A) (...) (C) (D)

III. Matching
1. D.
2. F.
3. A.
4. G.
5. J.
6. H.
7. B.
8. I.
9. E.
10. C.

IV. Vocabulary
1. M.
2. N.
3. P.
4. D.
5. H.
6. Q.
7. I.
8. F.
9. O.
10. A.
11. L.
12. G.
13. J.
14. K.
15. T.
16. E.
17. C.
18. B.
19. R.
20. S.

ANSWER SHEET KEY - *Mythology*
Multiple Choice Unit Test 2

I. Matching	III. Matching	IV. Vocabulary
1. F.	1. D.	1. D.
2. B.	2. C.	2. A.
3. I.	3. G.	3. M.
4. G.	4. J.	4. O.
5. C.	5. F.	5. H.
6. J.	6. B.	6. C.
7. E.	7. A.	7. Q.
8. H.	8. I.	8. T.
9. A.	9. B.	9. K.
10. D.	10. E.	10. S.

II. Multiple Choice

1. (A) (...) (C) (D)
2. (...) (B) (C) (D)
3. (A) (B) (C) (...)
4. (...) (B) (C) (D)
5. (A) (B) (C) (...)
6. (A) (B) (...) (D)
7. (A) (B) (...) (D)
8. (A) (B) (...) (D)
9. (...) (B) (C) (D)
10. (A) (B) (C) (...)

11. P.
12. I.
13. G.
14. R.
15. E.
16. N.
17. L.
18. B.
19. J.
20. F.

UNIT RESOURCE MATERIALS

BULLETIN BOARD IDEAS - *Mythology*

1. Save one corner of the board for the best of students' *Mythology* writing assignments. Draw an outline of Mount Olympus the size of the space you have reserved. Put a caption such as YOU'RE THE TOPS! Or WRITING OF CHAMPIONS at the top of the bulletin board.

2. Take one of the word search puzzles from the extra activities packet and with a marker copy it over in a large size on the bulletin board. Write the clue words to find to one side. Invite students prior to and after class to find the words and circle them on the bulletin board.

3. Have students think of modern-day popular figures who seem to have characteristics similar to one of the deities or heroes. Find a picture of the person and glue it to a sheet of construction paper or poster board. Put the person's name and the name of the deity or hero on the paper. Include a list of similar characteristics.

4. Invite students to help make an interactive bulletin board quiz. Give each student a half-sheet of paper (about 4" x 5"), folded in half so that it can open. On the outside flap, have each student write a description of one of the characters in the text. On the inside, they will write the name of the character. You can staple or tack these papers to the bulletin board so that the students can read the descriptions and lift the flaps to find the answers.

5. Collect pictures of the flowers mentioned in Chapter 4, *Flower Myths* and make a display of them.

6. Make a display of pictures of constellations and planets named for the deities and heroes.

7. On the left side of the board, place a Greek-style house (either drawn or cut out.) Above it, place the words PRINCIPAL GODS. Across the board, place similar houses labeled DESCENDANTS OF PROMETHEUS, ANCESTORS OF PERSEUS and HERCULES, ANCESTORS OF ACHILLES, THE HOUSE OF TROY, THE HOUSE OF ATHENS, and THE HOUSE OF THEBES. Put small cards with the names of the characters in an envelope at the bottom of the bulletin board. Encourage students to place the cards in the appropriate houses. Students may want to refer to the family trees at the back of the book.

8. Make a display of travel posters of Greece and Scandinavia.

9. Invite students to help you collect pictures of the deities and heroes, and display them on the bulletin board.

10. Have students design postcards depicting the settings of the myths.

EXTRA ACTIVITIES - *Mythology*

One of the difficulties in teaching a novel is that all students don't read at the same speed. One student who likes to read may take the book home and finish it in a day or two. Sometimes a few students finish the in-class assignments early. The problem, then, is finding suitable extra activities for students.

One thing that helps is to keep a little library in the classroom. For this unit on *Mythology,* you might check out from the school or public library other books by Edith Hamilton. A biography of Hamilton would be interesting for some students. There are also other retellings of the various myths which students may find interesting. Your more advanced students may enjoy reading some of the original sources cited in Hamilton's work (Aeschylus, Homer, Euripides, etc.) You may also want to include books about the mythologies of other cultures not covered in Hamilton's *Mythology.* Try to include some easy to read children's books and picture books for your less-able readers and ESL students. There are several mythology texts available for children, and these have very good illustrations that will aid the comprehension of these students.

Other things you may keep on hand are word search puzzles. Several puzzles relating directly to *Mythology* are included in the unit. Feel free to duplicate them.

Some students may like to draw. You might devise a contest or allow some extra-credit grade for students who draw characters or scenes from *Mythology*. Note, too, that if the students do not want to keep their drawings you may pick up some extra bulletin board materials this way. If you have a contest and you supply the prize, you could, possibly, make the drawing itself a non-refundable entry fee.

Have maps, globe, and travel brochures on hand for easy reference. Travel agencies and automobile clubs are good sources for these materials.

The pages which follow contain games, puzzles, and worksheets. The keys, when appropriate, immediately follow the puzzle or worksheet. There are two main groups of activities: one group for the unit; that is, generally relating to the *Mythology* text, and another group of activities related strictly to the *Mythology* vocabulary.

Directions for the games, puzzles, and worksheets are self-explanatory. The object here is to provide you with extra materials you may use in any way you choose.

MORE ACTIVITIES - *Mythology*

1. Pick one of the stories for students to dramatize. Encourage students to write dialog for the characters. (Perhaps you could assign various stories to different groups of students so more than one story could be acted and more students could participate.) The brief sketches in Part Five, *The Great Families of Mythology* would work well here.

2. Have students design a book cover (front and back and inside flaps) for *Mythology*.

3. Have students design a bulletin board (ready to be put up; not just sketched) for *Mythology*.

4. Invite a story teller to tell one or more creation myths or other stories related to *Mythology* to the class.

5. Use some of the related topics (noted earlier for an in-class library) as topics for research, reports, or written papers, or as topics for guest speakers.

6. Have students create a *Mythology Times* newspaper. Assign teams of students to write news articles based on one of the myths. An editorial team could review the articles, and a production team could publish the newspaper.

7. Help students design and produce a talk show. Choose one of the myths as the topic. The host will interview the various characters. (Students should make up the questions they want the host to ask the characters.) Some of the longer stories, such as the *Trojan War, The Adventures of Odysseus,* or *The Adventures of Aeneas* would work well here.

8. Have students work in pairs to create an interview with one of the gods or goddesses. One student should be the interviewer and the other should be the god or goddess. Students can work together to compose questions for the interviewer to ask. Each pair of students could present their interview to the class.

9. Invite students who have read other versions of the myths to give short book talks, and compare and contrast Hamilton's work with that of other authors.

10. Design a new land for Odysseus to visit. Describe the people or creatures, the location of the country, and the physical characteristics of the country. Describe how Odysseus got there, what he did while he was there, how long he stayed, and how he left. This project could also be done for Jason, Aeneas, Perseus, or Theseus.

11. Brainstorm ways for Odysseus to use his time now that his journeys have come to an end.

MORE ACTIVITIES - *Mythology* continued

12. Devise more labors for Hercules to perform.

13. Design a new monster. Give it a name, and describe its origin. Tell what it does. Draw a picture or make a model of it out of clay or papier-mache.

14. Have students find modern-day references to the gods. (EX: the names of the planets, automobiles, companies, sayings.) Make a class list of any that are found.

15. Assist students in writing a Reader's Theater script for one of the myths. Students could perform the short play for the class.

Mythology Word Search

```
A D E M E T E R W O O D E N D P M Y G
C O R I O N A S I R A P E K I S F U
H L V N T T U J N I R N C B A Y D N N
I Z H H H N Z O L P C P Y A N C A N D
L L S E O P S I S O A O L Q A H S A R
L Y N R R A D U R M R L K E R E I U
E A C C J A S P A T A F F O I D X S N
S T C U R A Q Z O H F J T M E A S Y J
V R H L G R O N L S L C Z M T D D L J
H E L E N N S A D B E S U A L E N E M
R M P S S U V R R H E I K Q M W N X S
K H G C P E S C A R C A D I V D K E E
C V Q I H G U I G G E E E O A C N X M
D I D O O U F S S O A H C I N H Z V R
S E E S M N R S A Y L R R P C I E J E
O Y L C E N E U S F P A X A K R U L H
X M P K R A Y S I P B H R W N O S W A
Z I H T Y R A N I D O A U A E N E A S
Y R I T I T A N S K D O T S I L L A C
```

ACHILLES	DELPHI	HELEN	NIFLHEIM	SISYPHUS
AENEAS	DEMETER	HERA	ODIN	THESEUS
AMAZONS	DIANA	HERCULES	OEDIPUS	THOR
ARACHNE	DIDO	HERMES	ORION	TITANS
ARIADNE	ELYSIAN	HOMER	PARIS	TROY
ASGARD	FLEECE	ILIAD	PEGASUS	TYR
ATHENA	FREYA	JASON	PLEIADES	VALHALLA
CALLISTO	GUNDRUN	MEDEA	POSEIDON	WOODEN
CHAOS	GUNNAR	MENELAUS	PROCNE	YMIR
CHIRON	HECTOR	MIDAS	PSYCHE	ZEUS
CRONUS	HELA	NARCISSUS	RHEA	

Mythology Word Search Answer Key

ACHILLES	DELPHI	HELEN	NIFLHEIM	SISYPHUS
AENEAS	DEMETER	HERA	ODIN	THESEUS
AMAZONS	DIANA	HERCULES	OEDIPUS	THOR
ARACHNE	DIDO	HERMES	ORION	TITANS
ARIADNE	ELYSIAN	HOMER	PARIS	TROY
ASGARD	FLEECE	ILIAD	PEGASUS	TYR
ATHENA	FREYA	JASON	PLEIADES	VALHALLA
CALLISTO	GUNDRUN	MEDEA	POSEIDON	WOODEN
CHAOS	GUNNAR	MENELAUS	PROCNE	YMIR
CHIRON	HECTOR	MIDAS	PSYCHE	ZEUS
CRONUS	HELA	NARCISSUS	RHEA	

Mythology Crossword

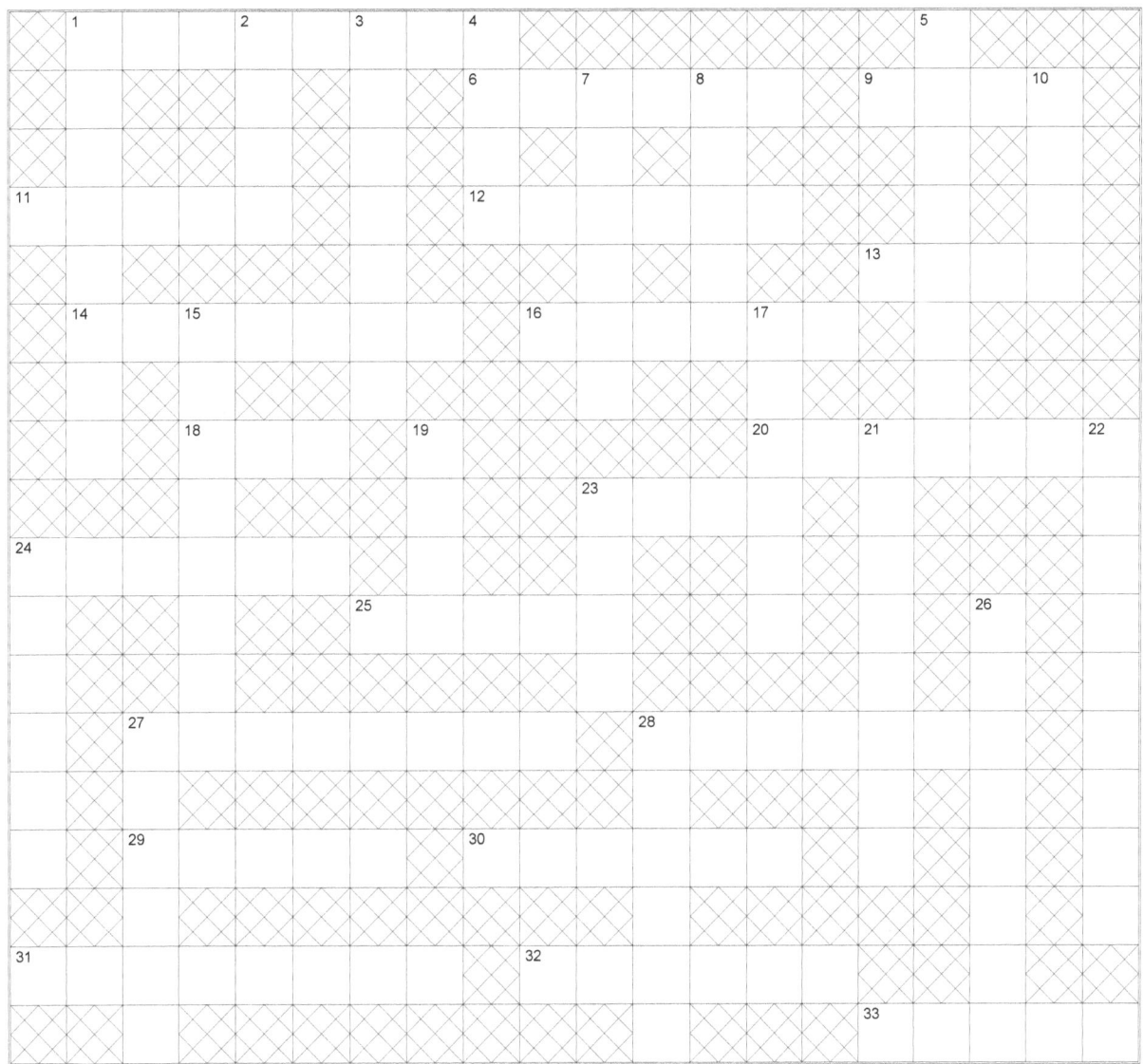

Across
1. Half bull, half human
6. Killed in battle with Achilles
9. Besieged city
11. Wife of Menelaus, kidnapped by Paris
12. Loved by Persephone and Aphrodite
13. God of Thunder
14. Weaver turned into a spider
16. His brother killed Sigurd
18. Tuesday was named for him
20. Married Sigurd
23. Ruler of Niflheim
24. Wife of Odin
25. Author of the Iliad and Odyssey
27. Guard-dog of the Underworld
28. Made Athens a commonwealth
29. First written record of Greece
30. Vesta, Goddess of the Hearth
31. God of Wine
32. Founder of the Roman race
33. First hero in Europe who undertook a great journey

Down
1. Husband of Helen
2. Solemn, aloof god
3. Helped Theseus escape from Labyrinth
4. Mother of Zeus
5. Put to sleep as a punishment
7. Titan father of Zeus
8. Hunter placed in sky as a constellation
10. Killed by Odin
15. Buried her dead brother
17. Home of Norse gods
19. Founded Carthage
21. Norse Underworld
22. Fell in love with his reflection in a pool
23. Wife of Zeus, Protector of Marriage
24. Golden ____ was the object of Jason's quest
26. Rolled a rock forever uphill
27. Centaur who trained sons of heroes
28. Elder Gods

Mythology Crossword Answer Key

	1 M	I	2 N	O	3 T	4 A	U	R			5 B		
	E		D		R	6 H	7 C	8 T	O	R	9 T	R	10 Y
	N		I		I	E	R	R			Y		M
11 H	E	L	E	N	A	12 A	D	O	N	I	S	N		I
L					D			N		O		13 T	H	O	R
	14 A	15 R	A	C	H	N	E	16 G	U	N	N	17 A	R	
	U		N			E			S			S			L
	S		18 T	Y	R		19 D				20 G	U	21 N	D	R	U	22 N
			I				I		23 H	E	L	A		I			A
24 F	R	I	G	G	A		D		E			R		F			R
L			O			25 H	O	M	E	R		D		L	26 S		C
E			N						A			H		I		I
E		27 C	E	R	B	E	R	U	S		28 T	H	E	S	E	U	S
C		H									I			I		Y	S
E		29 I	L	I	A	D		30 H	E	S	T	I	A		M		P	U
		R									A					H	S
31 D	I	O	N	Y	S	U	S		32 A	E	N	E	A	S		U	
		N									S		33 J	A	S	O	N

Across
1. Half bull, half human
6. Killed in battle with Achilles
9. Besieged city
11. Wife of Menelaus, kidnapped by Paris
12. Loved by Persephone and Aphrodite
13. God of Thunder
14. Weaver turned into a spider
16. His brother killed Sigurd
18. Tuesday was named for him
20. Married Sigurd
23. Ruler of Niflheim
24. Wife of Odin
25. Author of the Iliad and Odyssey
27. Guard-dog of the Underworld
28. Made Athens a commonwealth
29. First written record of Greece
30. Vesta, Goddess of the Hearth
31. God of Wine
32. Founder of the Roman race
33. First hero in Europe who undertook a great journey

Down
1. Husband of Helen
2. Solemn, aloof god
3. Helped Theseus escape from Labyrinth
4. Mother of Zeus
5. Put to sleep as a punishment
7. Titan father of Zeus
8. Hunter placed in sky as a constellation
10. Killed by Odin
15. Buried her dead brother
17. Home of Norse gods
19. Founded Carthage
21. Norse Underworld
22. Fell in love with his reflection in a pool
23. Wife of Zeus, Protector of Marriage
24. Golden ____ was the object of Jason's quest
26. Rolled a rock forever uphill
27. Centaur who trained sons of heroes
28. Elder Gods

MATCHING QUIZ WORKSHEET 1 - *Mythology*

____ 1. Achilles   A. had a vulnerable heel

____ 2. Cronus   B. bound to a rock while eagle ate his liver

____ 3. Chaos   C. Artemis, the Chief Huntsman

____ 4. Theogony   D. author of Iliad and Odyssey

____ 5. Diana   E. asked for golden touch

____ 6. Delphi   F. ten year journey after Trojan War

____ 7. Aeneas   G. Titan father of Zeus

____ 8. Odin   H. solemn, aloof god

____ 9. Ymir   I. rolled a rock uphill forever

____ 10. Rhea   J. account of creation of the universe and gods

____ 11. Odysseus   K. mother of Zeus

____ 12. Prometheus   L. Location of Apollo's oracle

____ 13. Signy   M. killed herself after brother killed her family

____ 14. Hercules   N. formless confusion at beginning of world

____ 15. Midas   O. defied Creon to bury her brother

____ 16. Telemachus   P. son of Odysseus

____ 17. Sisyphus   Q. guard-dog of Underworld

____ 18. Cerberus   R. performed twelve labors as penance

____ 19. Antigone   S. killed by Odin

____ 20. Homer   T. founder of the Roman race

ANSWER KEY MATCHING QUIZ WORKSHEET 1 - *Mythology*

A.	1.	Achilles	A.	had a vulnerable heel
G.	2.	Cronus	B.	bound to a rock while eagle ate his liver
N.	3.	Chaos	C.	Artemis, the Chief Huntsman
J.	4.	Theogony	D.	author of Iliad and Odyssey
C.	5.	Diana	E.	asked for golden touch
L.	6.	Delphi	F.	ten year journey after Trojan War
T.	7.	Aeneas	G.	Titan father of Zeus
H.	8.	Odin	H.	solemn, aloof god
S.	9.	Ymir	I.	rolled a rock uphill forever
K.	10.	Rhea	J.	account of creation of the universe and gods
F.	11.	Odysseus	K.	mother of Zeus
B.	12.	Prometheus	L.	Location of Apollo's oracle
M.	13.	Signy	M.	killed herself after brother killed her family
R.	14.	Hercules	N.	formless confusion at beginning of world
E.	15.	Midas	O.	defied Creon to bury her brother
P.	16.	Telemachus	P.	son of Odysseus
I.	17.	Sisyphus	Q.	guard-dog of Underworld
Q.	18.	Cerberus	R.	performed twelve labors as penance
O.	19.	Antigone	S.	killed by Odin
D.	20.	Homer	T.	founder of the Roman race

MATCHING QUIZ   WORKSHEET 2 - *Mythology*

____ 1. Athena   A. gave man the gift of fire

____ 2. Hephaestus   B. distracted by three golden apples

____ 3. Hermes   C. place of blessedness where good were rewarded

____ 4. Elysian fields D. Norse Underworld

____ 5. Persephone   E. became wife of Cupid

____ 6. Demeter   F. first tamer of horses for man's use

____ 7. Dionysus   G. rode Pegasus to kill the Chimaera

____ 8. Prometheus   H. center of belief in immortality

____ 9. Pandora   I. killed his sister's family for revenge

____ 10. Paris   J. created to punish men

____ 11. Adonis   K. Vulcan, God of Fire

____ 12. Psyche   L. warrior daughters of Harmony and Ares

____ 13. Amazons   M. Mercury, winged messenger of gods

____ 14. Bellerophon   N. loved by Aphrodite and Persephone

____ 15. Ariadne   O. Goddess of the Corn

____ 16. Atalanta   P. home of Norse gods

____ 17. Valhalla   Q. his judgment caused the Trojan War

____ 18. Asgard   R. helped Theseus escape from labyrinth

____ 19. Sigmund   S. hall for Norsemen who died bravely

____ 20. Niflheim   T. lived on Earth and in Underworld

ANSWER KEY MATCHING QUIZ   WORSHEET 2 - *Mythology*

F. 1.	Athena	A.	gave man the gift of fire
K. 2.	Hephaestus	B.	distracted by three golden apples
M. 3.	Hermes	C.	place of blessedness where the good were rewarded
C. 4.	Elysian fields	D.	Norse Underworld
T. 5.	Persephone	E.	became wife of Cupid
O. 6.	Demeter	F.	first tamer of horses for man's use
H. 7.	Dionysus	G.	rode Pegasus to kill the Chimaera
A. 8.	Prometheus	H.	center of belief in immortality
J. 9.	Pandora	I.	killed his sister's family for revenge
Q. 10.	Paris	J.	created to punish men
N. 11.	Adonis	K.	Vulcan, God of Fire
E. 12.	Psyche	L.	warrior daughters of Harmony and Ares
L. 13.	Amazons	M.	Mercury, winged messenger of gods
G. 14.	Bellerophon	N.	loved by Aphrodite and Persephone
R. 15.	Ariadne	O.	Goddess of the Corn
B. 16.	Atalanta	P.	home of Norse gods
S. 17.	Valhalla	Q.	his judgment caused the Trojan War
P. 18.	Asgard	R.	helped Theseus escape from labyrinth
I. 19.	Sigmund	S.	hall for Norsemen who died bravely
D. 20.	Niflheim	T.	lived on Earth and in Underworld

REVIEW GAME CLUE SHEET - *Mythology*

SCRAMBLED	WORD	CLUE
SAECLHLI	ACHILLES	had a vulnerable heel
SADNIO	ADONIS	loved by Persephone and Aphrodite
SEANAE	AENEAS	founder of the Roman race
NOMENGAMA	AGAMEMNON	sacrificed his daughter
ZANOSAM	AMAZONS	warrior daughters of Harmony and Ares
NOTNAGIE	ANTIGONE	buried her dead brother
CREANHA	ARACHNE	weaver turned into a spider
RAINEDA	ARIADNE	helped Theseus escape from Labyrinth
GRADSA	ASGARD	home of Norse gods
NAATLAAT	ATALANTA	married winner of footrace
TNAEHA	ATHENA	sprang full-grown from Zeus' head
CUBSHAC	BACCHUS	another name for Dionysus
NERBOELHPOL	BELLEROPHON	rode Pegasus to kill Chimaera
NBDYLRIH	BRYNHILD	put to sleep as punishment
LOCALSIT	CALLISTO	put in the sky as the Great Bear constellation
SREEBRUC	CERBERUS	guard-dog of the Underworld
HOSAC	CHAOS	immeasurable abyss at the beginning
HCORNI	CHIRON	Centaur who trained sons of heroes
UONRSC	CRONUS	Titan father of Zeus
PLOYCSC	CYCLOPS	one-eyed monster
LEADSAUD	DAEDALUS	creator of Labyrinth
PEDILH	DELPHI	location of Apollo's oracle
TREEMED	DEMETER	Goddess of the Corn
ANDAI	DIANA	Artemis, the Chief Huntsman
DIOD	DIDO	founded Carthage
SOYUNIDS	DIONYSUS	God of Wine
YEARF	FREYA	Norse Goddess of Love and Beauty
GRAFIG	FRIGGA	wife of Odin
NGRUUND	GUNDRUN	married Sigurd
NRGNAU	GUNNAR	his brother killed Sigurd
THORCE	HECTOR	killed in battle with Achilles
LEAH	HELA	ruler of Niflheim
NLEEH	HELEN	wife of Menelaus, kidnapped by Paris
PUHSASTEHE	HEPHAESTUS	Vulcan, God of Fire
AHRE	HERA	wife of Zeus, Protector of Marriage
LERCHESU	HERCULES	performed twelve labors as a penance
MHSEER	HERMES	Mercury, winged messenger of the gods

THISAE	HESTIA	Vesta, Goddess of the Hearth
MOREH	HOMER	author of the *Iliad* and the *Odyssey*
RIUSAC	ICARUS	flew too close to the sun
ALDII	ILIAD	first written record of Greece
HAIGIPENI	IPHIGENIA	sacrificed by Agamemnon for strong winds
NOASJ	JASON	first hero in Europe who undertook a great journey
BIRHATYNL	LABYRINTH	prison for Minotaur
DEEAM	MEDEA	helped Jason
LEANSEUM	MENELAUS	husband of Helen
DAIMS	MIDAS	wished for golden touch
DRIDAMG	MIDGARD	battlefield for men after death
ORMTIUAN	MINOTAUR	half bull, half human
SASRUNCSI	NARCISSUS	fell in love with his reflection in a pool
LIMEFIHN	NIFLHEIM	Norse Underworld
DION	ODIN	solemn, aloof god
SOYSUSED	ODYSSEUS	had ten year journey after Trojan War
PESIDUO	OEDIPUS	killed his father and married his mother
NORIO	ORION	hunter placed in sky as a constellation
DRANOPA	PANDORA	opened box of harmful things
RASIP	PARIS	kidnapped Helen
AGESSUP	PEGASUS	winged horse
EELNEPOP	PENELOPE	faithful wife of Odysseus
SEPRHEENOP	PERSEPHONE	lived on Earth and in Underworld
LIMEAHOPL	PHILOMELA	wove her story into a tapestry
EDEPASIL	PLEIADES	seven daughters of Atlas
LEPCONISYE	POLYNEICES	Creon refused him burial
SINEODOP	POSEIDON	Neptune, God of the Sea
CRONEP	PROCNE	changed into a nightingale
HOMRTEUESP	PROMETHEUS	gave man the gift of fire
CSEYHP	PSYCHE	married Cupid
NOILGYAMP	PYGMALION	fell in love with a statue
HEAR	RHEA	mother of Zeus
MISNUGD	SIGMUND	killed his sister's husband and children
YINGS	SIGNY	killed herself after her family was killed
DISRUG	SIGURD	rescued Brynhild from a ring of fire
SPUYHISS	SISYPHUS	rolled a rock forever uphill
ATASNUTL	TANTALUS	couldn't reach food or drink
MALESECHUT	TELEMACHUS	son of Odysseus
GOONHETY	THEOGONY	account of the creation of the universe and the gods
HUESSET	THESEUS	made Athens a commonwealth
ROTH	THOR	God of Thunder

AINTTS	TITANS	Elder Gods
ORYT	TROY	besieged city
RTY	TYR	Tuesday was named for him
LAVAALHL	VALHALLA	Hall of the Slain
RIMY	YMIR	killed by Odin
SUEZ	ZEUS	Jupiter, chief god

VOCABULARY RESOURCE MATERIALS

Mythology Vocabulary Word Search

```
R E V I V E D R C I T I F E D P T H F
S E Q K S T D E D P F N V K R O E Y A
T T M W E F E N C L P D Z O A A T P L
E U Z O N K R D R U W I F V C C H N C
B B M Z T E E I C M G G N O K H E O O
P E L N I E D T S A C N C R E I R T N
E R R X N J N I X G A I R P T N E I E
D S I T E K O O B E C T W F E G D Z R
F G N B L Q P N M L H Y E O E D D E K
O N G N I D N U O S E R S I R E D M
R T E D I O U S B T O P P A D M E C V
A S N O L A T G A C L R W E S T E Q Z
G T I N D E R L I P E O C S A B M D V
E R O X C G I O O E T N U R N E P C K
G L U S J T U R N N O P E F G L H A H
O O S B N S T I U C M B T O U L A V P
R A G E Z I N O L U J Q O R I O T O D
G M V Y C G J U R V G L Y U N W I R D
E C Q O S A S S A F R A S M E S C T R
```

BELLOWS	FEROCIOUS	LOAM	RENDITION	TALONS
BERATED	FORAGE	PLUMAGE	RESOUNDING	TEDIOUS
CACHE	FORUM	POACHING	REVIVED	TETHERED
CAVORT	GLORIOUS	PONDERED	RUMPUS	TINDER
CITIFED	GORGE	PORTICO	SANGUINE	TOY
CONCEDED	GRUB	PREENING	SASSAFRAS	TUBERS
EDIBLE	HYPNOTIZED	PROVOKE	SENTINEL	UNTOWARD
EMPHATIC	INDIGNITY	RACKETEER	SIRED	VENTILATE
FALCONER	INGENIOUS	REMOTE	STEEPED	WORMED

Mythology Vocabulary Word Search Answer Key

```
R E V I V E D   R   C I T I F E D   P   T   H   F
S   S     D   E     P       N     K   R   O   E   Y   A
T   E     E   E     L       D     O   A   A   T   P   L
E M   N     D   N     U       I     V   C   C   H   N   C
E O     T     E   D   I     M       G     E   K   H   E   O   O
P   S     I     T     D     O     A     N     R   E   I   R   N
E       I     L         N     P     B     I     T     W   P   E   D   Z   E
D   S             E           O       L   H     Y   F     D     E   E   R
F       I           N         I     S     O       D   M
O       G N   I   D   O   S       R   S       R       E
R       T E D I O U S     T       O   W P   A       D     M
A       S   N   O L A T G A     C       R W   E     S       B       D
G       T   I   N D E R L   I   O     E O     C   S   A   M       C
E       R   O                 U       O     N     U   R   N   P       A
G       L   U         T   U   R       N     O   B   F E     G     H       V
O       O S     B   N S T I   U       C     M     T O     U   L       A
R       A         E       I N O           U       Y   R I     O       O
G       M   V     C     G   U         R             U   N     W       R
E               O   S A S S A F R A S   M       E       S       C       T
```

BELLOWS   FEROCIOUS   LOAM   RENDITION   TALONS

BERATED   FORAGE   PLUMAGE   RESOUNDING   TEDIOUS

CACHE   FORUM   POACHING   REVIVED   TETHERED

CAVORT   GLORIOUS   PONDERED   RUMPUS   TINDER

CITIFED   GORGE   PORTICO   SANGUINE   TOY

CONCEDED   GRUB   PREENING   SASSAFRAS   TUBERS

EDIBLE   HYPNOTIZED   PROVOKE   SENTINEL   UNTOWARD

EMPHATIC   INDIGNITY   RACKETEER   SIRED   VENTILATE

FALCONER   INGENIOUS   REMOTE   STEEPED   WORMED

Mythology Vocabulary Crossword

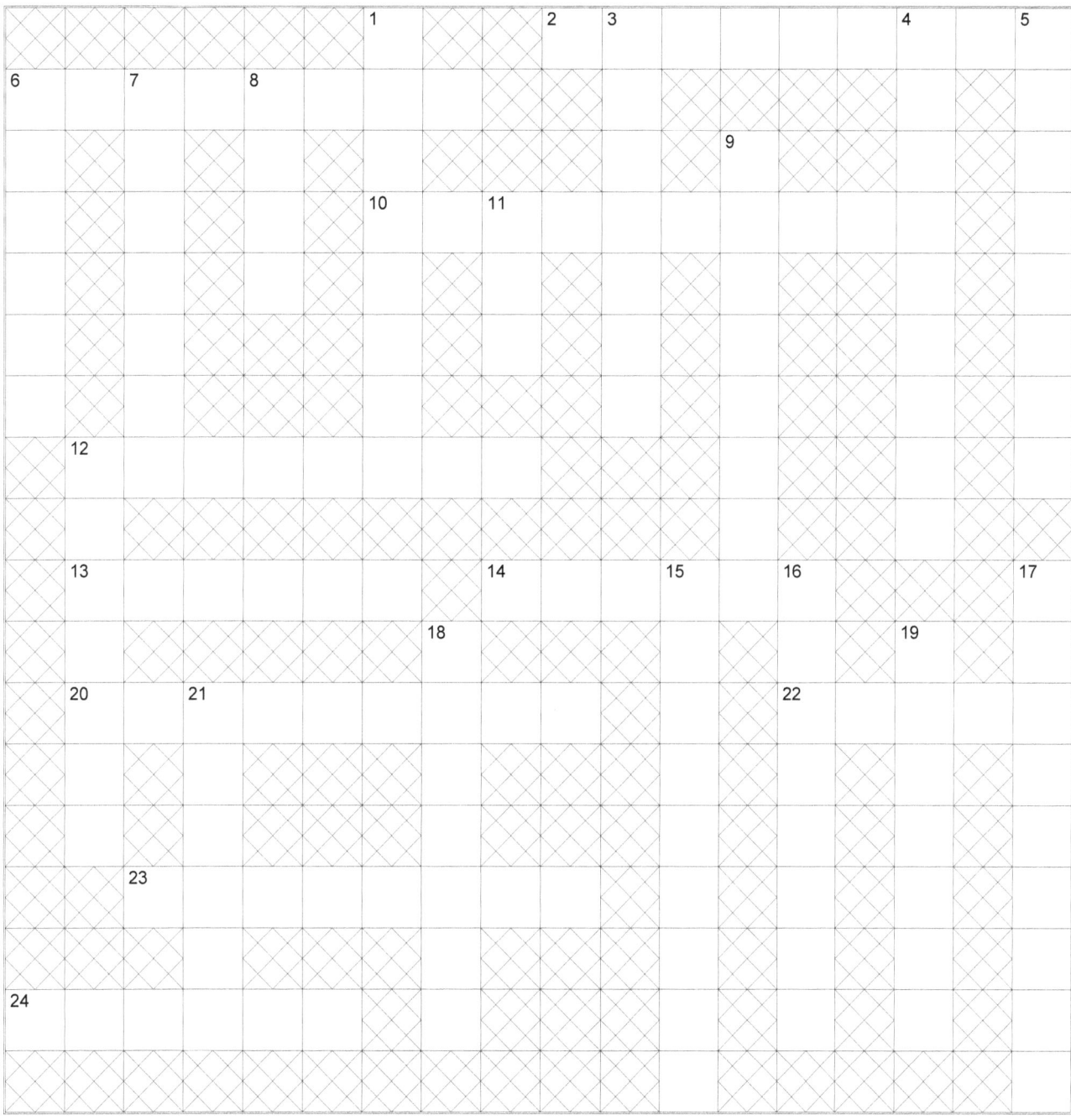

Across
2. prehistoric
6. leaning over as if to fall
10. able to secure
12. gave in
13. claws
14. crawled
20. secretly
22. fathered
23. movement; speed
24. underground stems which bear buds

Down
1. unfortunate
3. brought back to a healthy state
4. clever; inventive
5. definitely
6. material used to catch a spark
7. elaorate doorway
8. loose soil
9. passionate
11. play with; jest
12. having city habits
15. act of leaving one region for another
16. discouraged
17. offensive to pride
18. scolded harshly
19. stir to action
21. far away

Mythology Vocabulary Crossword Answer Key

						1 U		2 P	3 R	I	M	I	T	4 I	V	5 E
6 T	O	7 P	P	8 L	I	N	G		E					N		M
I		O		O		T			V			9 S		G		P
N		R		A	10 O	B	11 T	A	I	N	A	B	L	E		H
D		T		M	W		O		V			N		N		A
E		I			A		Y		E			G		I		T
R		C			R				D			U		O		I
	12 C	O	N	C	E	D	E	D				I		U		C
	I											N		S		
	13 T	A	L	O	N	S		14 W	O	15 R	M	16 E	D			17 I
	I				18 B					I		I		19 P		N
	20 F	U	21 R	T	I	V	E	L	Y		G		22 S	I	R	E D
	E		E				R				R		M		O		I
	D		M				A				A		A		V		G
		23 M	O	M	E	N	T	U	M		T		Y		O		N
			T				E				I		E		K		I
24 T	U	B	E	R	S		D				O		D		E		T
											N						Y

Across
2. prehistoric
6. leaning over as if to fall
10. able to secure
12. gave in
13. claws
14. crawled
20. secretly
22. fathered
23. movement; speed
24. underground stems which bear buds

Down
1. unfortunate
3. brought back to a healthy state
4. clever; inventive
5. definitely
6. material used to catch a spark
7. elaborate doorway
8. loose soil
9. passionate
11. play with; jest
12. having city habits
15. act of leaving one region for another
16. discouraged
17. offensive to pride
18. scolded harshly
19. stir to action
21. far away

VOCABULARY WORKSHEET 1 - *Mythology*

____ 1. nymph

____ 2. redoubtable

____ 3. disdainful

____ 4. pedestrian

____ 5. portent

____ 6. lamentation

____ 7. destitute

____ 8. dauntless

____ 9. diligent

____ 10. infallibly

____ 11. promontory

____ 12. satyrs

____ 13. arbiter

____ 14. prodigy

____ 15. plausible

____ 16. pliant

____ 17. abashed

____ 18. prototype

____ 19. exonerate

____ 20. endowments

A. human-like creature with goat's horns, ears, legs

B. fearless, not intimidated

C. ordinary, not imaginative

D. sign, forewarning, omen

E. to free from blame

F. a person who has exceptional talents or powers

G. a female spirit that represents nature

H. funds donated to a group or individual

I. impoverished, lacking the means of subsistence

J. an original that serves as a model

K. marked by careful, persistent effort

L. arousing fear or awe

M. embarrassed

N. a high ridge of land that juts out into the water

O. showing contempt

P. having some truth, but still open to doubt

Q. not capable of an error

R. song or poem expressing grief or mourning

S. easily bent

T. a judge

ANSWER KEY VOCABULARY WORKSHEET 1 - *Mythology*

G. 1. nymph   A. human-like creature with goat's horns, ears, legs

L. 2. redoubtable   B. fearless, not intimidated

O. 3. disdainful   C. ordinary, not imaginative

C. 4. pedestrian   D. sign, forewarning, omen

D. 5. portent   E. to free from blame

R. 6. lamentation   F. a person who has exceptional talents or powers

I. 7. destitute   G. a female spirit that represents nature

B. 8. dauntless   H. funds donated to a group or individual

K. 9. diligent   I. impoverished, lacking the means of subsistence

Q. 10. infallibly   J. an original that serves as a model

N. 11. promontory   K. marked by careful, persistent effort

A. 12. satyrs   L. arousing fear or awe

T. 13. arbiter   M. embarrassed

F. 14. prodigy   N. a high ridge of land that juts out into the water

P. 15. plausible   O. showing contempt

S. 16. pliant   P. having some truth, but still open to doubt

M. 17. abashed   Q. not capable of an error

J. 18. prototype   R. song or poem expressing grief or mourning

E. 19. exonerate   S. easily bent

H. 20. endowments   T. a judge

VOCABULARY WORKSHEET 2 - *Mythology*

1. trivial, lacking in importance
    A. succored	B. incalculable	C. paltry	D. diligent
2. associating with
    A. consorting	B. exultant	C. discerning	D. scudding
3. not stained or tainted
    A. inexorable	B. unsullied	C. pliant	D. diligent
4. absurd, incongruous
    A. contemptible	B. dauntless	C. ludicrous	D. enamored
5. to consent without protest
    A. exonerate	B. circumvent	C. tryst	D. acquiesce
6. the supporting of life or health
    A. sustenance	B. audacity	C. futility	D. atonement
7. embarrassed due to failure
    A. somber	B. sordid	C. suppliant	D. chagrined
8. skimming along swiftly and easily
    A. filial	B. scudding	C. susceptible	D. omniscient
9. clear, understandable
    A. omnipotent	B. desolate	C. manifest	D. inevitable
10. a turbulent or overwhelming flow
    A. torrent	B. tryst	C. oracle	D. rout
11. dirty from poverty or lack of care
    A. filial	B. susceptible	C. suppliant	D. squalid
12. severe, having no decoration
    A. plausible	B. austere	C. implacable	D. reputed
13. a fatal epidemic or disease
    A. pestilence	B. clamor	C. havoc	D. homage
14. perceiving as being different
    A. divination	B. expiating	C. discerning	D. incarnate
15. a prophet
    A. dryad	B. soothsayer	C. laggard	D. heifer
16. assisted, helped
    A. succored	B. wafted	C. loathed	D. ascribed
17. horribly, cruelly
    A. perpetually	B. eminently	C. sumptuously	D. atrociously
18. government representatives
    A. naiad	B. retinue	C. raiment	D. usurper
19. soothing, pacifying
    A. pedestrian	B. implacable	C. appeasing	D. reputed
20. unforgiving, seeking revenge
    A. vindictive	B. discerning	C. unsullied	D. inexorable

ANSWER KEY VOCABULARY WORKSHEET 2 - *Mythology*

C. 1. trivial, lacking in importance
    A. succored   B. incalculable   <u>C. paltry</u>   D. diligent

A. 2. associating with
    <u>A. consorting</u>   B. exultant   C. discerning   D. scudding

B. 3. not stained or tainted
    A. inexorable   <u>B. unsullied</u>   C. pliant   D. diligent

C. 4. absurd, incongruous
    A. contemptible   B. dauntless   <u>C. ludicrous</u>   D. enamored

D. 5. to consent without protest
    A. exonerate   B. circumvent   C. tryst   <u>D. acquiesce</u>

A. 6. the supporting of life or health
    <u>A. sustenance</u>   B. audacity   C. futility   D. atonement

D. 7. embarrassed due to failure
    A. somber   B. sordid   C. suppliant   <u>D. chagrined</u>

B. 8. skimming along swiftly and easily
    A. filial   <u>B. scudding</u>   C. susceptible   D. omniscient

C. 9. clear, understandable
    A. omnipotent   B. desolate   <u>C. manifest</u>   D. inevitable

A. 10. a turbulent or overwhelming flow
    <u>A. torrent</u>   B. tryst   C. oracle   D. rout

D. 11. dirty from poverty or lack of care
    A. filial   B. susceptible   C. suppliant   <u>D. squalid</u>

B. 12. severe, having no decoration
    A. plausible   <u>B. austere</u>   C. implacable   D. reputed

A. 13. a fatal epidemic or disease
    <u>A. pestilence</u>   B. clamor   C. havoc   D. homage

C. 14. perceiving as being different
    A. divination   B. expiating   <u>C. discerning</u>   D. incarnate

B. 15. a prophet
    A. dryad   <u>B. soothsayer</u>   C. laggard   D. heifer

A. 16. assisted, helped
    <u>A. succored</u>   B. wafted   C. loathed   D. ascribed

D. 17. horribly, cruelly
    A. perpetually   B. eminently   C. sumptuously   <u>D. atrociously</u>

B. 18. government representatives
    A. naiad   <u>B. retinue</u>   C. raiment   D. usurper

C. 19. soothing, pacifying
    A. pedestrian   B. implacable   <u>C. appeasing</u>   D. reputed

B. 20. unforgiving, seeking revenge
    <u>A. vindictive</u>   B. discerning   C. unsullied   D. inexorable

VOCABULARY REVIEW GAME - *Mythology*

SCRAMBLED	WORD	CLUE
SADBEAH	ABASHED	embarrassed
ECQAISUEC	ACQUIESCE	to consent without protest
TALACIUQT	ACQUITTAL	clearing from a charge or accusation
ARABSIOM	AMBROSIA	the food of the gods
SEPIAGANP	APPEASING	soothing, pacifying
BARTERI	ARBITER	a judge
IDSRABEC	ASCRIBED	attributed to
TENAMONET	ATONEMENT	making amends for an injury
UROCALOYSTI	ATROCIOUSLY	horribly, cruelly
DIUTAYCA	AUDACITY	daring, boldness
UTAESER	AUSTERE	severe, having no decoration
ROWEB	BOWER	a shaded, leafy recess or arbor
CSAEDCNE	CADENCES	balanced, rhythmic beats
AUPORICSIC	CAPRICIOUS	impulsive, given to whim
NADGCEHIR	CHAGRINED	embarrassed due to failure
MUCRICTNEV	CIRCUMVENT	to go around or bypass
COMRAL	CLAMOR	loud expression of discontent
SOSOLUCS	COLOSSUS	a huge statue
RNISGOONCT	CONSORTING	associating with
BONETPICTMEL	CONTEMPTIBLE	despicable
NSUESLATD	DAUNTLESS	fearless, not intimidated
FEEDIID	DEIFIED	worshipped as a god
TOESALED	DESOLATE	barren, lifeless
EDTEUSITT	DESTITUTE	impoverished
GLITEDIN	DILIGENT	marked by careful, persistent effort
GIRCINNESD	DISCERNING	distinguishing
AFDLSNIDUI	DISDAINFUL	showing contempt
VAIDOININT	DIVINATION	foretelling events by using the supernatural
DARYD	DRYAD	a wood nymph
NINETMYLE	EMINENTLY	outstanding, distinguished, of high quality
EMTUAL	EMULATE	to compete with successfully
RNDOEAME	ENAMORED	inspired with love
WENDONEMST	ENDOWMENTS	funds donated to a group or individual
CEEDITN	ENTICED	lured, tempted
NAXEORETE	EXONERATE	to free from blame
AGTNIIPXE	EXPIATING	making amends, atoning
TTXNUEAL	EXULTANT	joyful, triumphant

IFILAL	FILIAL	of a son or daughter
LUYITIFT	FUTILITY	frivolous, having no useful result
CHOA	HAVOC	devastation, chaos
AMOEHG	HOMAGE	honor or respect that is shown publicly
BLICAPEMLA	IMPLACABLE	not able to be appeased
DYEINALTERVTN	INADVERTENTLY	accidentally
EICLNUBALLAC	INCALCULABLE	unpredictable, impossible to foresee
CARTENANI	INCARNATE	given human form
EBTIEVNLAI	INEVITABLE	impossible to avoid
RNEAIBOXEL	INEXORABLE	not able to be persuaded
LLLFIIYNBA	INFALLIBLY	not capable of error
DRAGGAL	LAGGARD	straggler
NETMALIONAT	LAMENTATION	a song or poem that expresses grief
HEALDOT	LOATHED	detested
OLDCISUUR	LUDICROUS	absurd, incongruous
TSEFINAM	MANIFEST	clear, understandable
HYMOGYOLT	MYTHOLOGY	stories about the origin of the gods and heroes
AIDAN	NAIAD	a spirit that lives in brooks and streams
TRACEN	NECTAR	the drink of gods; undiluted juice of a fruit
PYHMN	NYMPH	a female spirit that represents nature
TIMENOTNOP	OMNIPOTENT	all-powerful
COTINEMNIS	OMNISCIENT	knowing everything
RACELO	ORACLE	the transmitter of prophecies at a shrine
TRAPYL	PALTRY	trivial, lacking in importance
DRAINSEEPT	PEDESTRIAN	ordinary, not imaginative
PREPLETLUYA	PERPETUALLY	lasting for an unlimited time
LICENSEPET	PESTILENCE	a fatal epidemic disease
BLASILUPE	PLAUSIBLE	having some truth, but open to doubt
TALIPN	PLIANT	easily bent
TROTPEN	PORTENT	sign, forewarning, omen
GROPYID	PRODIGY	a person with exceptional talents or powers
MYROOTONRP	PROMONTORY	land that juts out into the water
PETPYROOT	PROTOTYPE	an original that serves as a model
NITREAM	RAIMENT	clothing
UTRLEBDEAOB	REDOUBTABLE	arousing fear or awe
NOWREN	RENOWN	fame
DREEPUT	REPUTED	supposed, considered
EIRUTNE	RETINUE	messengers, government representatives

YRTSAS	SATYRS	part human, part goat
DUCNISGD	SCUDDING	skimming along swiftly and easily
SOBREM	SOMBER	gloomy, depressing
TOOHYESRAS	SOOTHSAYER	a prophet
DROIDS	SORDID	morally degraded
DAQIULS	SQUALID	dirty from poverty or lack of care
CRUDEOSC	SUCCORED	assisted, helped
GRAFEFUS	SUFFRAGE	the right to vote
USYUOLPUMST	SUMPTUOUSLY	lavishly, suggesting great expense
PLATPIUSN	SUPPLIANT	asking humbly
CESPSLTBEIU	SUSCEPTIBLE	easily affected or influenced
CANESNUTSE	SUSTENANCE	the supporting of life or health
ROTTERN	TORRENT	a turbulent or overwhelming flow
SYTRT	TRYST	a meeting arranged by lovers
TEMFUHNLOBAA	UNFATHOMABLE	not able to be understood
LUDNESILU	UNSULLIED	not stained or tainted
PURUSER	USURPER	one who takes another's place by force
INVITEDVIC	VINDICTIVE	unforgiving, seeking revenge
TOEVIV	VOTIVE	an offering to fulfill a vow
DEFATW	WAFTED	floated gently and smoothly

www.ingramcontent.com/pod-product-compliance
Lightning Source LLC
Chambersburg PA
CBHW051406070526
44584CB00023B/3309